THE
SELLING
STAIRCASE

MASTERING THE ART
OF RELATIONSHIP SELLING

NIKKI RAUSCH

THE
SELLING
STAIRCASE

Non-Fiction
Text copyright 2019 by Nikki Rausch

Any names, characters, places, events, incidents, similarities or resemblance to actual persons, living or dead, events, or places, are entirely coincidental.

Cover designed by Seedlings Online at www.seedlingsonline.com
Ebook production by E-books Done Right at www.ebooksdoneright.com
Typesetting by Atthis Arts at www.atthisarts.com

Visit www.yoursalesmaven.com for more information about the author, updates, or new books.

ISBN 9781072698784

THE
SELLING
STAIRCASE

For Stella, my bestie. You are a true blessing in my life. Thank you for your kindness, your love, and for always making me laugh.

Introduction

No Funnels Here

Have you ever heard of the sales funnel?

The concept of filling a sales funnel has been hammered into sales professionals by their bosses for years. Managers love to tell us, "You've got to fill your sales funnel." However, the concept—and what it takes to fill a sales funnel—is more about marketing your offer and bringing leads in the door. The sales funnel doesn't represent the actual sales process because the funnel gets people to tumble down toward your offer. It doesn't sell them on it.

Although filling a sales funnel is important, it doesn't represent what steps to take in order to earn someone's business.

When you're talking about authentic relationship selling, the best visual is a staircase. Think of it this way: once you have a lead interested in your business, your funnel disappears. At that point, many people find themselves standing there asking, "So they're here and interested . . . now what?"

It's *your* job to earn a client's business and move them through the steps toward the sale. If you don't know where you are on the staircase, you're going to miss a step. When a step is missed, your clients will stay where they are and never move. You're going to lose sales!

I want more for you.

That's why I'm presenting the Selling Staircase.

What is the Selling Staircase?

This book is a five-step approach to move your clients through an authentic sales process. We're going to go through these in-depth throughout the book.

1. Introduction
2. Create Curiosity
3. Discovery
4. Proposal
5. Closing

The goal of sharing the Selling Staircase framework is to bring new awareness about what you're doing and how to be even more effective in the sales process. Knowing how to communicate with your clients, recognize Buying Signals, and ask for the sale is crucial to the success of your business.

Why Does This Matter?

As a kid, did you ever try to jump up as many steps at a time as you could? Were you able to jump up two or even three steps? What would happen if you tried this today as an adult? Maybe you'd still be able to make the jump . . . but how likely are you to try?

In the selling process, people often put too much pressure on themselves to immediately close the sale after meeting a prospective client. Those are unrealistic expectations. It's like asking the client to jump up four steps from a standing position. They'll fear doing it, and they might seriously hurt themselves (or in this case, their business). Most likely they'll tell you to go kick rocks and walk away.

When you skip steps in the selling process, you risk breaking rapport, overwhelming a client, or coming off as pushy. Up until now, you may have unknowingly been asking your potential customers to jump stairs. No wonder they didn't buy! It's too far to go from A to D. You need to follow A with B, and B with C, etc. Earning someone's business is a step-by-step process.

Skipping steps can also be a product of one's feelings toward the sales process. For example, some people think sales are gross. This same group is usually focusing on themselves, not on the client. Sales is about the client, and the Selling Staircase ensures that the sale stays focused on the client, even if closing the sale might take a few minutes or a few years.

Regardless of how long it takes, it's your job to move your client one step up the staircase at a time to the sale. Don't expect them to move themselves—trust me, you'll be disappointed. And if your approach to sales is to *wait for people to tell you they're ready to buy before asking for the sale* . . . this book was written specifically for you.

What This Book Will Do

It will change the way you sell.

My intent is to give you a clear structure to follow so you're able to close more business. And more importantly, once you understand the structure of the sales conversation, you'll feel more at ease. You'll no longer try to sell like someone else. You'll be confident in your own skills, and your personality will shine through. This means more of your ideal clients will be drawn to working with you.

We're going to talk about the Selling Staircase, what the steps are, and help you understand what's working and what you're struggling with. You'll uncover what you need to do differently, and how to do it a better way.

The Selling Staircase will decrease the angst you feel about selling. When you understand the structure, and how to move someone to the next step, sales get so much easier.

In the Selling Staircase, I will provide you with all the tools you need to:

1. Know the steps.
2. Understand why they are important.
3. Know how to navigate each one.
4. Make selling easy.

As you go through the book, you will find several prompts where I ask you questions and encourage you to write responses in your own words. Take the time to work through each section and not simply skip those parts. Write in this book! Keep your notes with you as a guide when you make sales calls. Some of the concepts may appear in more than one chapter. That's intentional. Feel free to jump back and forth through the book if you require a refresher.

Allow yourself to discover what steps in your process might be missing, and learn how to incorporate them to increase the number of people who choose to work with you.

The Sales Maven Mission

The mission of my company is to teach you more effective ways to build rapport, communicate, sell, and grow your business. I have more than twenty years of experience working as an author, trainer, and award-winning sales executive behind me, selling to organizations such as the Bill & Melinda Gates Foundation, Johnson & Johnson, Hewlett Packard, Seattle Public Schools, and NASA.

I know my way around sales.

My master certification in Neuro-Linguistic Programming (NLP), and over 1,200 classroom hours studying it, gives me a special understanding of the link between the brain, the way we use language, and the body. I love to use my NLP background to teach business owners how to create authentic connection and build rapport with potential clients.

While you don't need over 10,000 hours of practice like I have to be effective at sales, it does take time and dedication to master the process of relationship selling using these steps. The tools compiled in this book will get you there much faster and put you ahead of your competition.

To grow your business by understanding and mastering the Selling Staircase, you're invited to continue reading.

CHAPTER 1
Step 1: Introductions

It all counts.

This phrase has stuck with me since first hearing it from my mentor regarding professional relationships. It has since become an integral part of the work I do with clients. Whenever you work with people, it all counts.

It all counts is especially true when it comes to introductions. You have likely heard about the power of first impressions. Would you be surprised to learn that it only takes 1/10 of a second for someone to decide if you are trustworthy?[1]

According to a 2016 article by Business Insider,[2] a bad first impression is nearly impossible to overcome. They say, "First impressions are a lot stickier than we're inclined to believe—and often they work like self-fulfilling prophecies."

Ways Introductions Happen

In the first 5-10 minutes of meeting a person, they are deciding, *do you have any value to me?* Introductions are a huge part of this value decision and setting first impressions, so it's important to make your introduction count. Fortunately, this isn't as difficult to do as it may seem. You can begin to prove your value through your introduction, which also makes a positive first impression.

Here are a few ways we're introduced to people:

- Going to an event

---

1 Baer, Drake. 2015. "Science Says People Decide These 13 Things within Seconds of Meeting You." Business Insider. Business Insider. November 18, 2015. http://www.businessinsider.com/science-of-first-impressions-2015-11.

2 Lebowitz, Shana. 2016. "Turns out It's Nearly Impossible to Get Past a Bad First Impression." Business Insider. Business Insider. December 12, 2016. https://www.businessinsider.com/first-impressions-matter-more-than-we-think-2016-12.

- Finding a new website
- Via email from a mutual acquaintance
- People that have already known you for years, but are just comprehending what you do.

Let's be honest; people are skeptics. I know I am! We want to make sure that the people we're giving our money to are credible. When selling, make sure that you show you are trustworthy by making a powerful introduction.

How to Make a Powerful Introduction

At first contact with another person, you want to instantly send the message that you are likable and credible in order to overcome skepticism.

Below are three things you can do to achieve this:

1. Say Your Name. When making introductions, do you say your name? For those who had an immediate "Yes, of course," response . . . are you sure?

Let's say an acquaintance introduces you to a person. Do you say your name to that person? It's shocking how often people don't tell you their name. It's common for people to introduce me to a group like this:

"Everyone, this is Nikki. Nikki, this is everyone." As I go around and shake hands with people, they might say, "Hi, it's nice to meet you." They rarely give me their name. I have to ask for it.

Even when I'm speaking at an event and get an introduction like, "Everyone this is Nikki," I still give my name to each person when I meet them individually. I never assume people know my name. I'll say, "Hi, I'm Nikki Rausch. It's nice to meet you."

Unfortunately, even *that* rarely gets people to give their name in return.

When I have to ask a person to tell me their name, an immediate impression is formed. I think to myself, "Oh, this person lacks social etiquette and professionalism." And right or wrong, it's unlikely that person will get my business. I prefer to work with professionals who understand social cues.

These simple social interactions matter.

Remember, people are making judgments about you. You have a short window of time to establish your credibility. Saying your name sets yourself up for success by making it easy for people to connect with you.

Even if your name has been announced to a room, still introduce yourself to individuals using your name. The worst that can happen in this situation is they hear your name twice. The best that can happen is they now feel a connection to you.

Now, It's your turn. Over the next week, introduce yourself to five people you don't know. Be sure to say your name, and take note of how often they give their name in return. Record the occurrence and whether or not you got their name in the space below.

_____

_____

_____

_____

_____

Bonus Tip! For those who, like me, feel shy in a room full of new people, here's a simple technique to keep you engaged: act as if this is your event. As the host, it's your job to make others feel comfortable. One way you might do this is by making introductions. Take someone you've met before, and introduce them to someone brand new. This raises your credibility in the room. People will remember you as someone who went out of their way to make them feel comfortable.

2. Don't Say This. There is a right and a wrong approach to talking about your uniqueness in an introduction. Unfortunately, I see the wrong approach all too often. It confuses prospects, and it turns people off.

Before I share the wrong approach, I'm going to make a quick request: *do not picture a blue zebra in your head.* Don't imagine how the vibrant blue color stands out from the black stripes.

Be honest; do you now have a blue zebra in mind?

I said not to picture the blue zebra, so why do you have a clear mental image of a blue zebra?

When people tell you not to think about something, you automatically start to think about it. And when salespeople tell you all the things they don't do, do you get a mental picture of those very things in your mind?

Too many people start off their elevator pitch by listing the things they don't do. Here's an example:

"My company is Sales Maven. I'm a sales coach. I'm different than most sales coaches because I don't give people scripts, dictate how many calls they need to make each day, or set how many people they must meet to hit their sales goals. I also don't spend time analyzing clients' current sales data to recommend what they need to change."

The real issue with this approach is that I never actually told you what I do. Ok, time to be honest. It's just you, inside your head. Do you do this? If you do—stop. You might assume that when you tell people what you don't do, they'll make the connection to what you actually do.

It doesn't work that way.

You're asking too much of people. You should always give a succinct description of what you do so prospects are able to quickly understand how they'll benefit from your product/service.

Now, it's your turn. Let's get specific on what you do that makes you unique. Give clear examples demonstrating your product or service when asked, "What do you do?" Use the space below to decide what you'll say:

_____

_____

_____

_____

_____

3. Give Answers Clients Understand. When you learn something for the first time, have you ever noticed you often recall a similar experience from your past to help you make sense of the new information?

This is known as association, and it is the basis for all memory and learning.

When you teach a toddler how to open a few types of doorknobs, they will quickly be able to associate that movement to any type of doorknob. (Much to the chagrin of their parents!)

Understanding association and how to use it is an effective selling tool to help your clients learn about your product/service. The mistake many business professionals make is they inhibit association by not giving their prospective client-specific information.

Here are some examples. Which do you think are more effective for helping clients make associations?

Example 1A: I'm a financial planner, helping people with money.

Example 1B: As a financial planner, I help clients wanting to retire before the age of 55.

Example 2A: My products improve people's overall health and well-being.

Example 2B: One of the advantages clients report after taking my product is that they no longer feel exhausted at 3:00 pm. They maintain their energy throughout the full workday, are more productive, and have more fun.

Example 3A: The advantage of being a VIP client is the sessions are specific to your business.

Example 3B: Each VIP client receives tailor-made sessions for their business. For example, in one VIP session, we were able to map out the client's traditional selling cycle. By making small tweaks to the process and the language my client was using, we reduced the selling cycle from four meetings to one before getting a signed contract. This resulted in my client closing $8,000 in new business within two weeks of our first session.

When I coach my clients on this, the objection I almost always hear is, "But Nikki, if I give a specific example, people will assume that's all I do!"

Let me clear something up: you are not missing out on business by using associations.

When someone says they help people retire before the age of 55, do you assume they can't help you with your 401K? Probably not. You associate and wonder how their service would apply to you. It's easier for clients to make the jump to how your product or service applies to them when you give them something specific to start with.

Talking in general terms burdens the prospect to come up with their own example before associating your product/service to their need. It's your job to make it easy for the client to understand what you do and how you might help them—not theirs. They shouldn't have to work that hard.

Frankly, they won't.

Now, it's your turn. In the workbook area below, write down a specific example you can use when talking about your product or service to make it easy for clients to associate your service with their need.

_____

_____

_____

_____

_____

Judging at a Glance

Whether we like it or not, the cold, hard truth is we all judge others. It has been scientifically proven time and again.

Think back to the last time you were in a networking meeting with lots of people you'd never met before. Did you scan the room to find someone you'd like to get to know or perhaps flag the people you wouldn't approach with a 10-foot pole?

Have you ever wondered what people think when they see you at these events? What vibes are you giving off with your clothes, mannerisms, tone of voice, and other nonverbal cues? These subtle aspects of how you present yourself are often overlooked opportunities. They can draw people to you or push them away.

Everything you do and say (in addition what you wear) makes a statement. *It all counts* includes paying close attention to how you show up and the impression you're making on those around you. Every aspect of how you appear should help build a positive first impression.

Now, it's your turn. Think back to a networking event you attended where you didn't know anyone. Try to remember someone you saw in your scan of the room that made you say, "Nope! Not going there!"

What was it about this person that made you want to avoid them? Write your answer in the space below.

_____

_____

_____

_____

_____

_____

At that same event, you likely ended up going and talking to some people.

1. What made you choose them?
2. Did they choose you?
3. What made this group or person more inviting?
4. How did they make you feel comfortable?

I've provided a workbook area for you to put your answers below.

1. _____

_____

_____

2. _____

_____

_____

3. _____

_____

_____

4. _____

_____

_____

Next, think about yourself when you attend an event where you do not know anyone.

1. What impression are you giving off?
2. Do people come talk to you?

1. _____

_____

_____

_____

2. _____

_____

_____

_____

Then consider an event where you knew a lot of people.

1. Do you have cliques of friends you immediately talk to while ignoring everyone else?
2. Do you seek out those who are new and uncomfortable and invite them into the conversation?

1. _____

_____

_____

_____

2. _____

_____

_____

_____

With all of these questions, I want you to ask yourself one final question: what can you do to be better at the next event? (We all have room to improve!)

_____

_____

_____

_____

_____

You've made introductions, sparked conversation with a prospective client, and walked them up the first step in the Selling Staircase. Now you must hold their attention to keep ascending the staircase by creating curiosity.

CHAPTER 2
Step 2: Creating Curiosity

Creating curiosity means tailoring what you say to match the interests of the person you're in a conversation with. This, in turn, encourages that person to ask questions.

Most people struggle with this step.

A lot of people think they aren't good closers in the selling process when actually their true problem is that they don't know how to create curiosity. If you don't know how to create curiosity, you likely don't get to talk about your business, which means you're walking away from a lot of ideal clients. They just never get the memo that you're the perfect professional to meet their need.

You can create curiosity anywhere—conferences, networking events, social gatherings, even while standing in line with people to order your coffee.

How to Create Curiosity

Let's go through how to create curiosity with a four-part example.

1. Open the Conversation with Permission

Ask someone, "Is it okay to ask about you and what you do?"

When you say, "is it okay to ask," watch their body language. You may notice that they're already nodding their head *yes*, even though they don't know what you're going to ask!

The implicit tone of the phrase "is it okay to ask" is the key here. When a person flatly says, "Tell me what you do for a living," that statement may come off as aggressive, and that doesn't help rapport. Asking first neutralizes this problem.

Then, once the person answers your question, pause and wait. Their next response is likely to ask you the same question you just posed to them. You now have permission to talk about what *you* do.

2. Take A Little Control

If they don't ask what you do, just continue on with the conversation. Sometimes this happens, and that's all right. However, if you're finding that all you do is ask questions and let other people talk about themselves, you'll never talk about your business. You need to take a little bit of control. Otherwise, you're missing out on opportunities to earn ideal clients!

The person asking questions in a conversation holds the power. You don't want to be the person asking all of the questions, and you don't want to be the person providing all the answers. You need to make sure there's a balance. Imbalance causes potential clients to buy from your competitors because they won't respect you, don't feel they know you, or think you come off as too aggressive.

The conversation should be reciprocal and have a good back and forth. I won't deny it—always asking questions feels safe. It's a way to keep from being vulnerable. That, however, means it is up to the answering party to feel vulnerable all the time. They might feel as if they're on the witness stand! Not allowing people to ask you questions also puts up a barrier. If you don't let people ask you questions, you may come across as guarded. People want to do business with those they know, like, and trust. You've got to give people the opportunity to get to know you.

You might be thinking to yourself, "That's all fine, but every time I attend events, people only talk about themselves. They never ask me questions, even if I pause and leave time for it." When this happens, there is something you can say to prompt an opportunity to talk about yourself.

Here's the language you might use:

"It's been so interesting to learn about you and your business! I'm wondering if you might be interested to learn a little bit about me and what I do?"

What you do with your voice when using this language is critical. These two sentences can potentially come off as shaming, right? We never want to make anybody feel like, *I just got corrected in some way*, or *I should've been asking that already.*

When I start this particular prompt by saying, "It's been so interesting to learn about you and your business," my shoulders come up. My body language changes. I divert my gaze. Then, when I finish with, "I'm wondering if you might be interested to learn a little bit about me and what I do," my head tilts slightly to the side, and I curl my voice up at "what I do."

There are some subtle cues being sent here. Body language wise, you use these changes to send the message: *I'm not shaming. I'm just wondering if you're interested. I'm legitimately curious if you'd be interested to learn about me and what I do.*

After delivering this prompt, I wait.

More than likely they're going to reciprocate and say, "Tell me a little bit about you and what you do?"

This is when it's your turn to share, which takes us to our next step.

By the way, if you'd like a video of me delivering this prompt, you can visit this page on my website.[3]

3. Decide What You Know

The potential client now wants to know what you do. Before you answer them, ask yourself, "What do I already know about this

---

3   To see the video, please visit: www.yoursalesmaven.com/sellingstaircasebonus

person?" You're going to tailor your answer to what you suspect may be relevant to them.

Of course, you might not know a lot about them. Keep in mind that just being there means that you do know *some* things.

You know where you are (physical location) with this person. You've probably seen and heard about them while at that location. You know what they're wearing, if they have an accent. Pay attention to their body language as well. What have they already said about their life situation?

Taking all of the information you've obtained in that short amount of time, respond with an answer that will interest them.

Here's an example. If I'm talking to somebody I know offers consulting services, I might say, "Service-based providers hire me to refine their discovery and consultation process so they can quickly identify who their ideal clients are and increase their overall close rate on those calls."

For a product-based person, I might say, "Businesses hire me to show them how to increase their overall sales per customer. As a result, they're able to ramp up their average selling price, grow their revenue quicker, and build long-term customer loyalty."

These are all answers I decide upon in the span of a moment since they need to be specific to the person I'm talking to. Be aware that they're asking a very simple question. You should have a straightforward answer. One time I got on a call with somebody, and I asked her, "Tell me a little bit about your background and what you do."

She talked for forty minutes.

She went through every single thing that had happened to her up until the present day. At the end of the forty minutes, I couldn't wait to get off the phone with her. I felt afraid to ask her another question because she'd word-vomited all over me!

Give a simple answer. In the curiosity phase, you *should not be pitching*. You're giving them enough information to see if it piques their interest. This is not an opportunity for you to explain your business in great detail. Your response should be no more than two or three sentences.

4. Wait

Once I give my answer, I wait to see if they have a follow-up question.

If somebody says, "Oh, that's nice. So how about our recent weather?" they're probably not that interested in learning more about you or your business. If they do have follow-up questions, a lot of times those come in the form of Buying Signals, which we'll discuss a little later.

Now, it's your turn.

Imagine a past interaction you had with someone at an event. Pretend they said, "Tell me a little bit about you and what you do." Ask yourself, *what do I already know about this person?* After considering the knowledge you have of them, write down a few answers in the workbook space provided below.

_____

_____

_____

_____

Dog-Calling and Cat-Calling

One of the ways I teach creating curiosity is to compare how people call a dog, versus how they call a cat.

When somebody calls a dog, they do so in a really high-pitched, aggressive voice. You often hear people say in an excited voice, "Come here, boy! Come here!" Dogs respond to that. They may think something fun is going on and run to their owner.

Most people are excited about what they do or sell. When they show up in a conversation excited to talk about their products/

services, they show up with dog-calling energy. It often comes across as either aggressive or pushy. That's never okay.

When people learn about dog-calling energy, they'll often justify it by saying, "That's just me and my style. People have to deal with it." Unfortunately, when that's your attitude, people won't just "deal with it." They'll avoid you!

Instead, think about how you call a cat. It's quieter, calmer. More of a "here kitty, kitty." A cat hears that and looks around. They may lean in to give you their full attention so they don't miss anything. Your answers to a potential client's questions should have a little bit of a "here, kitty, kitty."

Respond in a way that is interesting and allows the person to ask you a follow-up question. For example, you can prepare an answer to the very simple, basic question that we all get asked multiple times a week.

"How are you?"

What do you say? Do you have a very generic answer? "Oh, I'm fine." Or maybe you have a fun answer. "Oh, I'm living the dream!"

Neither of those answers allow for follow-up questions. If somebody asked me, "How are you?" I might say, "I'm fantastic. I just came back from speaking at an amazing event for women business owners."

This allows them to ask, "What did you speak about?" or "What was the conference about?" Now I get to talk more about who I am and what I do.

I work with clients on creating their "here kitty, kitty" responses all the time. My group coaching program participants practice their "here kitty, kitty" responses with each other to get feedback so they can continue to refine them. They frequently share how they have more opportunities to talk about their businesses and ultimately book more clients this way. They move people through this step in the Selling Staircase by practicing their "here kitty, kitty" responses.

Now, it's your turn.

Take a few minutes to write down your response to this question: "How are you?" in the workbook area below. How can you respond in a way that opens the door for someone to ask you a follow-up question? Keep in mind, this is not the time to word vomit on someone. Give a short answer. The best way to know if your "here kitty, kitty" response worked is to see if you get asked a follow-up question. If you're not getting follow-up questions, you need to refine your response.

_____

_____

_____

_____

All About Mascara

Here's a deeper dive into curiosity with some more examples.

Example 1: A client of mine used to struggle with getting people in her community to be interested in her business. Then she started changing her language during conversations to spark curiosity.

Before the change, if a prospect had asked my client: "How's your week going?"

The standard answer she would have given would be: "It's been good. How's your week going?" Her moment to spark curiosity would end there.

After she changed her answer to create curiosity, however, she might have said something like, "My week's been great, and it's been all about mascara." This is her "here kitty, kitty" response.

What do you think the prospect might have said next? Maybe something like, "What does that mean?"

That question gives my client a tiny window (permission) to talk about her business. "We just launched a brand-new mascara that women are going crazy for. It's my new favorite product, and that's all any of my clients want to talk about right now."

After that response, if her prospect was curious about this new mascara, she'd ask for more information. She may even want to place an order for herself. However, if she changes the subject, chances are she's not interested to know more.

That's okay. In those instances, we should be happy to spend time building rapport and strengthening the relationship.

Example 2: Let's say my service is teaching people skills to increase their sales/business. (Oh, yeah, that's what I actually do!)

This example is from an actual phone conversation I had. A woman I met at a networking event called me out of the blue. She said she's new to the area and looking to connect with people. She asked me how long I'd been a part of the networking group associated with the event.

Here was my response: "I've been a part of the group for less than a year. I got involved with them because a chapter opened up in my area. I've stayed involved with the group because I've met some amazing people, and I've been asked to speak at four of the chapters across the country."

Can you guess what she asked next?

She wanted to know the topic I spoke on. I could have answered her initial question by saying, "I've been a member since September." Unfortunately, that answer doesn't do anything to create curiosity.

By taking the question and expanding on it just a little bit, I've opened the door to see if she might be interested to know more about my business. She very well could have said, "That's nice. I just joined in February." If that had been the case, the conversation would have gone in a completely different direction. Which, by the way, would have been okay.

You know that saying, *if you do what you've always done, you'll get what you've always got?*

Maybe you're ready for something different? Maybe you'd like to start talking more about your business and what you offer? Here's your chance.

Now, it's your turn.

What are some "here kitty, kitty" responses that you can say to create curiosity? Write them in the workbook space below.

_____

_____

_____

_____

Buying Signals

Curiosity creates Buying Signals, which indicate that people are ready to move to the next step on the Selling Staircase with you. I hear them *everywhere*! They come up in the most and least obvious places that you would ever imagine.

Here's the trick: you have to act on the Buying Signal in the moment. Before I talk about how to act on them, let's first define a Buying Signal.

What is a Buying Signal?

A Buying Signal is an indication from your prospective client that they're interested in your product/service. They can be verbal or non-verbal. It's important to be on the lookout for them so you can act immediately when one shows up. The moment you receive a Buying Signal is the best time to invite someone to do business with you or move to the next step in the Selling Staircase.

If this seems difficult or scary to you now, not to worry. I am confident that after learning how to recognize and act on Buying Signals, you'll no longer feel it's acceptable to just hand someone your business card and hope they call you.

A Buying Signal can be as obvious as someone coming up and saying, "Hey, can I buy from you?" Chances are you don't need to read a book to recognize such an obvious one. Unfortunately, clients aren't usually so transparent as to say things like, "Please take my money," or "I'm ready to buy now."

Many times, the signals are much more subtle.

Examples of Buying Signals

My book *Buying Signals*[4] has seventeen examples of common Buying Signals. I will share the five here that best illustrate transitioning from curiosity to the next step on the Selling Staircase. Some are painfully obvious, and some are the ones that give my clients the most trouble. They are, in no particular order:

1. Asking about pricing
2. Asking for a discount (my favorite)
3. Bringing up a negative experience with a previous provider
4. Making positive comments (most overlooked)
5. Taking out his/her calendar, credit card, or another form of payment

Again, I hope you looked over this list and thought, "These seem pretty obvious." That goes to show how easy it should be to start picking up on them, right?

Maybe.

The truth is, many of these signals are missed so often by business owners it would shock you. Why is that?

The number one reason these Buying Signals are missed is because

---

4   Interested in reading Buying Signals? Visit https://yoursalesmaven.com/buying-signals/

they don't often appear in obvious ways. It was after noticing how often people were missing Buying Signals that I decided to write that book. If you're waiting around for your client to beg you to take their money, you'll be waiting a long time. It's not uncommon for someone to approach me at speaking opportunities to share how many new clients they've gained after learning how to recognize Buying Signals.

Let's talk about each Buying Signal individually.

1. Asking About Pricing

Here's one where you may be thinking to yourself, "Duh, this one's so obvious; I'd never miss it." Let me give you an example of this where it isn't quite so obvious.

A client of mine needed advice on how to handle a situation in a networking group. On two separate occasions, after my client gave a thirty-second elevator pitch, another woman in the group had approached her. The woman would appear with a hand on her hip and, in particularly aggressive tone of voice, ask, "How much do you charge for your service?"

My client shared with me how she was feeling judged by this woman and didn't quite know how to respond. She felt the woman was demeaning her in some way by her body language and tone when she asked about her pricing.

My response: "This sounds like a Buying Signal. Have you invited her to work with you?"

My client was shocked. In an incredulous voice, she replied, "Nikki, you should hear the way she asks the question."

"One of two things will happen," I said, "When you give her your price and then invite her to schedule a time to work with you, she'll either become a client, or she'll stop asking what you charge. It's a win-win either way for you. You'll have a new client, or you can spend your time connecting with other prospective clients at the event."

Fast forward a month, and the woman with the tone stands up at our networking event raving about my client and the service she received. Turns out, it was a Buying Signal. She was simply waiting to be invited to become a paying client.

Again, inviting a customer to do business with you after they ask about price might sound like a no-brainer. That's why you should always be open to hearing the price question. The way a potential client asks might not always be familiar, and you don't want to miss an opportunity.

2. Asking for a Discount

Many business owners worry that if a client asks for a discount and they tell them "no," they'll lose the sale. This has rarely been the case in my experience.

Even when a client asks for a discount, and you decline, you should still invite them to do business with you.

We have a culture of consumers programmed to expect discounts, sales, or clearance offers. It's common practice for people to ask for a discount. I mean, it never hurts to ask, right? When a client asks you for a discount, and you are unable or unwilling to offer one, assume they want to buy from you regardless of your answer.

I had a client call me frustrated because a customer had scheduled an appointment, then sent an email asking for a discount with a list of reasons justifying one. She mentioned her hours had been cut back at her job, she saw an ad for a competitor offering a lower price, and her husband was concerned about her spending money on the service.

When I asked my client if she wanted to offer a discount, she said, "No. I'd hate to lose her business, but I can't afford to offer what she's asking for."

We crafted an email response where my client expressed how excited she was to work with the customer and all the benefits she'd receive at her scheduled appointment.

Not only did the customer keep the appointment, but she ended up making the largest individual order my client had received up to that point in her business.

So, when clients ask for a discount, even if you are unwilling to provide one, take the chance and invite them to do business with you. You might be surprised at how often you still earn the business.

3. Negative Experiences

A few years back, I was asked to be the keynote speaker at a company's national sales convention. During my speech, I spoke about Buying Signals. Negative experiences was on the list. There were 90+ sales professionals in the room. When I put the slide up on the screen stating that a negative experience with a previous provider is a potential Buying Signal, there was a collective groan in the room.

When I asked why they were groaning, they said things like,

"That's the worst!"

"I hate it when that happens."

"I never know what to say."

In response, I explained that when people bring up a negative experience, they're looking for reassurance that working with you will be different.

Don't despair over the negative experience. Be willing to stay in the conversation. You might say, "I'm so sorry you had a bad experience in the past. If you'd be willing to consider working with me, I can assure you that your experience this time around will be much different. Here's how . . ."

When a client brings up a negative experience, let them know they have nothing to fear. Then tell them what you do, or share a story about what others have experienced with you. Make sure your examples demonstrate positive experiences that counter what the prospect went through in the past. Then, invite them to do business with you.

You may be surprised at how often people are willing to give you a shot when you reassure them of how you'll take care of them.

4. Making Positive Comments

This is probably the most overlooked Buying Signal I come across. When someone goes out of their way to give you a compliment about your product/service, be appreciative, and then invite them to do business with you.

Let me give you an example:

A few years ago, I met a lovely woman at a networking event, and we set up a date to meet for coffee. While at coffee she asked me about what services I offer at my company, Sales Maven.

When I shared what I did, she said, "That's so interesting. I know a few people who would benefit from working with you."

Ding, ding, ding! That's the sound I hear in my head when I am presented with a potential Buying Signal.

My response to her was, "Thank you. I would so appreciate if you'd be willing to make an introduction to the people you think would benefit from my work." I then said, "Now, how about you? Is this something you might be interested in as well?"

Her response was, "Nikki, I've been in sales for twenty years. I don't need help with sales." The conversation then shifted to another topic.

A few weeks later, she registered for one of my complimentary classes. Afterwards, she reached out to me and said, "Nikki, I didn't think I could learn anything new about sales, and yet I did in your class. Your approach is so different from the traditional sales training I've had in the past."

Positive comment—*ding, ding, ding!* A possible Buying Signal.

I thanked her for her compliment and then invited her to sign up for a course I was teaching. Her response was, "I don't really think that course is for me. However, I might like to work with you privately."

We scheduled a strategy session, and at the end of the session she said, "Wow, I got a lot out of today, and I think there's more I could learn from you." *Ding, ding, ding*—another positive comment.

I invited her again to participate in a course of mine centered around what she wanted to learn. She declined.

A few months later, she showed up at a class I was teaching for a networking group. She sat in the front row, directly in front of me. It just so happened the training I taught that night was the same training I had given a few months back in the free class she participated in.

At the end of the training, the first thing she said to me was, "Nikki, I want to learn to speak like you."

Ding, ding, ding. Positive comment and potential Buying Signal number three!

I said, "Thank you; that's so kind. You know my course is about to start, and in it I teach a whole section on language skills. You're warmly invited to be a part of this group." She told me she'd started a new job and didn't have time for the course. I offered to work with her privately, and she declined.

Later, when I arrived back to my office, I had an email from her that said, "I can't stop thinking about what I learned from you tonight, and I want more. I'm in for your course. Call me tomorrow, and I'll give you my credit card to pay the tuition."

Let's review.

Every time she made a positive comment, I invited her to work with me. She told me *no* multiple times before she ever said *yes*. And that's ok. I was willing to build the relationship and invite her to do business every time I heard a Buying Signal.

This is an example of a convincer strategy. Your convincer strategy changes based on the context. Rest assured, you have one. My convincer strategy is usually about three interactions. If I have some interest in something, I usually have to hear about it three times before I'm ready to take the next step.

Now, it's your turn. Start to notice your own convincer strategy by answering these questions in the space provided below. How many times did you have to hear about this book before you decided to purchase it? How about before you decided to start reading it?

_____

_____

_____

_____

_____

Your current prospective clients are no different than you. You may have not hit their convincer strategy yet, so be willing to invest in the relationship with them. And when they give you a Buying Signal, kindly invite them to do business with you—even if they have said *no* to you in the past.

5. Taking Out Their Calendar, Credit Card, or Other Form of Payment

When I hear a potential client say to a business owner, "I'd like to schedule a time to work with you," and the business owner responds, "Give me a call, and we'll get a time scheduled," while handing over a business card, I want to bang my head on a table.

This is one of the biggest crimes against Buying Signals and pains me the most.

When a client asks to schedule time to work with you with, schedule the appointment on the spot. When you hand someone a business card and say, "Call me," you risk never hearing from the person again.

It's not that the client loses interest. It's more likely that they get busy and distracted. After talking to you, they have voicemails to listen to, emails to return, social media to engage in, meal plans to finalize, kids to drive to soccer practice, and the list goes on and on.

You want to catch people when their interest in working with you is at its highest. This Buying Signal is one of those times. Take the ninety seconds to schedule with them or place their order. Remember, it's your job to make it easy for your clients to work with you.

I once told a woman I wanted to order her product. She gave me her business card and told me to call her next week. I was floored. She had a ready customer, and she blew me off.

Did I call her the following week? Nope. I placed my order with a vendor selling the same product who was willing to take my business on the spot.

Recognizing Buying Signals is an important part of maintaining rapport. These subtle cues are clients telling you that they're ready to work with you! Acting on them will deepen their trust and your relationship.

Now, it's your turn. Think back and pinpoint up to five moments where someone gave you a Buying Signal, and you missed it. Make a list now in the workbook area below.

_____

_____

_____

_____

_____

Now circle back with the people on this list, and invite them to work with you.

Ask for the Sale

At this point you may be asking, "How can I be sure the client is sending me a Buying Signal?" Here's how: invite the person to the logical next step. The next step may be scheduling a time for a discovery call or it may be placing an order.

If you ask, and the client says, "No, that's not for me," that's okay. Now the conversation can move on to something else. When they say, "Yes," then you know you received a Buying Signal. Capitalize on it!

There is no downside. In all my years in sales, I have never had anybody get offended by an invitation to do business. However, my chances of earning business always go up significantly when I do ask, and yours will too.

Sometimes, a prospective client may not realize they're interested in doing business with you. By inviting them to do business, you give them the opportunity to decide if they're ready to move forward.

The bottom line is this: any time there's even a hint of a Buying Signal, it's your duty to investigate by extending an invitation to do business with you.

I know, this may be coming off like a broken record at this point. The repetition is intentional so you can easily internalize it. A lot of the tips in this book are simple, and if you are willing to take the actions I suggest, your business will benefit.

Many clients have told me this one tip of inviting and asking has transformed their businesses. All of a sudden, they're signing up clients left and right. They're always surprised that it came from such a simple tweak. So, when it comes to Buying Signals, one rule trumps them all. Repeat it with me:

When you get a Buying Signal: Ask. For. The. Sale.

CHAPTER 3
Step 3: Discovery

The third step on the Selling Staircase, discovery, is about uncovering a client's biggest problem, struggle, or need. Doing this allows you to streamline the rest of the Selling Staircase and effectively provide the best product or service to meet that need.

This is not the time for a high-pressure sales pitch. You will diminish trust and rapport if you do that. Your goal during the discovery step is to make the process easy for your client and provide a safe place for open discussion. This allows them to be candid about their need, increasing your chances of having a successful discovery call. Remember, it's your job to put the client at ease from the start of the call.

Please note, if your client does not need a discovery/consultation call in order to place their order or hire you, *they* can skip this step. It's not ok for *you* to skip this step because you want to take their money. You risk damaging rapport or selling your client something that they will not be satisfied with. This will ultimately cost you the relationship, repeat business, and referrals. It's not worth it. So, set yourself up for long-term success and conduct discoveries.

Next, I'll share a crucial technique for setting yourself and your client up for a successful encounter.

Pre-framing

Your prospect may have some nerves about showing up to the call with you. They may have had consultations in the past where someone went into a hard sell. They may have walked away from calls ashamed or embarrassed. They may even feel intimidated by you, given you're an expert. To alleviate these feelings, you can set expectations or "pre-frame" at the beginning of a call.

Doing this not only gives them a benchmark for the current discussion; it creates safety for the potential client right at the beginning. Again, safety is key. If you miss it, that person may never relax with you.

Here is a language example on how to pre-frame. Change this up based on how you would frame a call.

Thank you so much for making time today to chat. We're scheduled to talk for thirty minutes.

The reason you give a timeframe is because they may have something scheduled after this, and you don't want them thinking about it. Let them know you are keeping track so they do not have to.

Next, go into permission.

Does this still fit in your schedule?

If they say *no*, then reschedule the call. If they say *yes*, great! It's time to state the purpose.

The purpose of this call is to find out a little bit more about you and how I may be a resource to you. With your permission, I'll start with a few quick questions. You're welcome to ask me questions at any point. At the end of our chat, we can discuss ways to work together if that makes sense for both of us.

Pause for a moment here, and then say,

Is it okay to ask you a few questions now?

The importance of getting permission during the Discovery process cannot be overstated. Be respectful and ask permission before you dive in.

In my NLP studies, we had a presupposition known as: *Pre-framing Is Worth A Ton of Reframing*. In other words, it's best to spend a few minutes at the start of a conversation letting the other person know what to expect (pre-framing). You don't want to leave people feeling blindsided and then have to backpedal to try to build back the rapport (reframing).

Here's an example of how one of my clients implemented this technique into her business: At the beginning of every client meeting, she pre-frames for them that, with permission, she'll be asking probing questions into their current financial position. If at any time, the client doesn't know the answer or feels uncomfortable sharing the information in the initial call, they can ask her to skip the question. This pre-frame lets her clients know she'll respect their privacy, and the rapport stays intact throughout the meeting.

She shared with me recently that her discovery meetings are going more smoothly, and clients are actually being more forthcoming with information. The best news is that she's closing more business as a result of a more refined process.

The perfect selling environment is when your client is at ease and feels a sense of security about what to expect.

Pre-framing your calls lets people take a breath and loosen nerves, establish expectations, and realize the meeting is focused on them. It also builds rapport. Let's look at an example where someone did not pre-frame or create safety.

Create Safety

I often share a story about a trusted colleague of mine when I talk about safety. They wanted to introduce me to a woman they knew and were adamant she would help my business.

We set up a time for me to meet this woman at a coffee shop and for us to get to know each other. She shows up late to the meeting. She sits down at my table, reaches into her bag, and pulls out a huge laptop. It's so big, I actually have to move my drink back so she doesn't tip it over.

She then says, "So, Sales Maven—tell me a little bit about your needs."

Then she launches into more questions. No pre-framing at all. Every time she asks me a question, and I give her an answer, she types it into her computer. By the sixth question, I'm starting to feel a little annoyed by the way she is handling this in-person discovery conversation.

The questions continue, and at one point, I ask, "What are you typing?"

She replies, "I'm typing up a proposal for you."

That's when I decide to be done. I say, "Really? On what?"

I hadn't given her permission to give me a proposal. I was completely outside any semblance of safety in the conversation. I ended the conversation as quickly and as gracefully as I could. I went back to my office, and she sent me a proposal later that day.

I didn't sign with her because she didn't do any pre-framing or create any safety for me. She just launched into her agenda. A discovery call isn't about *your* agenda. You should have *an* agenda, but the client should never feel like it's *your* agenda.

Let's go into this example a little further and talk about the mistakes she made.

Her first big mistake was asking questions during the discovery process that she only needed answers to once I agreed to hire her.

Now, you may be thinking, "Nikki, I need this information."

Yes, you'll need the information *eventually*, when they've hired you, and there's an opportunity for you to get it. This opportunity could be through an intake form, another scheduled call, or even on that same call after they hire you. If you're asking too many questions during the discovery call, you may be overwhelming people.

In the discovery process, all questions should lead to hiring you.

I have a VIP client who doesn't come from a sales background.

She was having these great introduction conversations with people at events. They were interested in her services. Then she would send them an email with a list of things they needed access to in order to schedule a discovery call with her. You might not be surprised to learn that people would then decline a discovery call.

I revealed to her that all of the stuff on her list was information the client would need after they hired her. She agreed, though remained adamant that they should have it ready during a discovery call to speed up the process. Unbeknownst to her, this was a subtle way of skipping the discovery step in favor of closing with a client. And people weren't willing to do it. Once she revised her intake process, clients began scheduling discovery calls, and she started closing more business.

Discovery calls are an opportunity to demonstrate your professional skills and provide a safe place for your clients to divulge their needs, wants, and struggles. Doing this will allow you to lead people seamlessly through the Selling Staircase and close more business.

One Grain of Sand

Salespeople will often try to coach during discovery calls. If this is something you do, I suggest stopping. You might be talking people out of working with you!

Here's an example. A potential client wants to question you about your professional knowledge. You agree, and they ask something that falls into the purview of your services.

In these cases, I would say, "You know what, that is actually something we would work on in a strategy session, so you let me know if that's something you're interested in talking about scheduling."

You are an expert in your profession. The information that you know is vast and comes very easily to you. Due to this, you might give potential clients a grain of sand during discovery calls in the form of information because you want to help them. It is just one grain of sand, and you have an entire beach available for them once they hire you.

All of us come from a place of service. You genuinely want to help others and do good work. The grain of sand you offered might help them and make a difference. To them, it is so much more. That one little grain of sand, to them, might be all they think they need in order to get their need met. You've opened a whole new world to them, and now they no longer think they need you. Because of that, they choose not to hire you.

By giving that nugget of information, you've done them a disservice because now they won't take the time to engage with your wealth of knowledge. Your wealth of knowledge is what is going to make the biggest impact in their lives. That grain of sand is just the first step in getting them moving in the right direction. They likely will stay stuck as a result of thinking they no longer need to hire you.

This is why I don't coach during discovery calls.

Too Many Questions

Remember my client who had the long list of required information for people to come prepared with for a discovery call? Not only was she trying to skip the discovery step in the Selling Staircase, she was also asking the client too many questions. This can cause the prospect to become overwhelmed. They might say things like, "I need to think about it." This stalls the sales process for you and delays the potential client from getting their needs met.

All questions have to lead to hiring you. Ask yourself, *what are the very specific questions that I need answers to in order to deliver a proposal/suggestion that demonstrates I can meet their need or solve their problem?*

When I get on a discovery call, I ask specific questions that relate to the work I do. I minimize the opportunity for the prospects to go off on tangents. If by the end, either I or the client determine that I am not the right person to help them, I bring the process to a close as quickly as possible and refer them to somebody else.

You should be closing 50% or more of your discovery calls. If you're struggling to convert your discovery calls, and each one is taking you an hour to conduct, chances are there's an issue with the questions you're asking. It is crucial to the success of both you and the prospective clients that you refine your questions.

What are some good questions to ask that would lead potential clients to hire you? A universal question that works in any industry is this: "What's important to you . . . (insert context relevant to your product/industry/services)."

For me, the question I ask is, "What's important to you this year regarding your sales goals?"

Not all questions should be cookie-cutter, however. Most need to be geared towards your skill set.

For instance, during one of my discovery calls I might ask, "How skilled are you at being able to create curiosity about your product or service?" I teach how to create curiosity about products or services. So, I make sure to insert a question that is useful to both discover the client's need *and* highlight that aspect of my business.

Remember, the discovery step isn't where you start selling! This is where you learn more about the client, and they learn about your process.

What is their problem?

Their need?

Their biggest want?

What you learn in the discovery call is the information you'll use to strategically lay out your offer once you move to the proposal step in the Selling Staircase. Doing a great job during the discovery step will make it easier for your client to say *yes* when you reach the closing step.

CHAPTER 4
Step 4: Proposal

The proposal step connects the client's needs with what you offer. You do this by either showing how your service will alleviate their struggles or how your product will meet their need. A well laid out proposal should allow the client to easily make a decision.

I cannot count the number of times I have heard stories of a client choosing not to purchase the perfect product for them due to a poorly delivered proposal. With many of these stories, the salesperson involved only needed to make a small tweak to their proposal! I want better for you. In this chapter, I'm going to make sure you don't run into that problem.

First, let's start with seven things you can do to strengthen your current proposal skills.

1. Asking Permission

Before launching into your offer, it is crucial to get permission again. If you simply say, "Here's why you should hire me," or "Here's what you should buy," you'll come across as pushy or aggressive. There's also no point in laying out a proposal if the client isn't interested.

Here is an example of asking for permission. The language here should be based on everything that you shared so far. "I see five key ways that we might work together. Are you interested in learning more about that?" Then, you wait and see what the client says.

If they say, "I'm not interested," it doesn't make sense for you to sell to them at that point. If you continue to push the sale, you'll definitely come across as pushy or aggressive. This may hurt your chances of their reaching out when they are ready to work with you. Be sure that you get permission before you launch into your proposal.

2. Responding to a "Yes"

When I go through the discovery phase, I write down key points of information about the potential client. Then, when I've gotten permission to lay out a proposal, I can look back over those notes. When I said, "Five key ways that we might work together" in the previous example, I'm more than likely looking at those key ways in my notes. Once I receive permission, I can confidently launch into my proposal.

Sometimes prospects will ask, "What are those five things, Nikki?" If this happens to you, don't decline to answer! You don't need to play your cards close to your chest. But, in this case, you'll want to tell them the "what", not the "how". Clients pay for the how.

For instance, when answering their questions about the five things, I might say, "The five areas we might work on to improve your selling skills are:

- Building rapport with people who have a different style than you,
- Creating curiosity so you have more opportunities to talk about your business,
- Recognizing Buying Signals and knowing what to say when you get one,
- Incorporating storytelling into the sales process, and
- Outlining an offer that makes it easier for a client to make a decision."

My clients sometimes say, "Well, if I give them the *what*, they can do the *how* on their own." Not true. If they really could do the *how* on their own, they'd already be doing it. They wouldn't need you, and they wouldn't value what you offer. So, don't be afraid of giving the *what* before they've paid you money.

3. Crafting the Proposal

When putting together a proposal, I recommend offering up to three possible options.

If you're thinking that you have twenty or more ways people can work with you, remember, you are the expert. It's your job to make recommendations based on the prospect's needs. Even if you have thirty ways somebody *can* work with you, you should be able to pare it down to three options that meet that client's needs based on your work in the discovery step. Three packages are enough to benefit most clients. Any more than three, and you may overwhelm the client with decisions.

4. Affordability vs. Need

Your proposals should not be based on what you think potential clients can afford. It's not your job to determine what a client can afford. Again, proposals should be based on the client's need.

When you go into a proposal, and you're making judgments about what somebody can afford, you're projecting a limiting belief. This can really hinder the relationship. Now, if a client tells you what their budget is, that may help narrow down your three options. The key here is to use their budget to select three options from *your existing packages*. Your offers should not totally change based on the client's budget. In general, if you don't have anything that fits in their budget, they're probably not a prospect.

I had a woman one time request private coaching from me because she was struggling to sell her hourly trainings. I had suggested working one-on-one because then I could really tailor all of my answers to her specific offering. She responded by asking how much she could get for $100. I suggested both of my books. I wasn't being flippant. I was being real. I don't work with clients privately for $100.

I want you to stand in your place of authority and expertise and be proud of your pricing. You don't have to discount based on what clients can afford. If they can't afford you, they're not a client. That's okay. They may actually figure out a way to afford you at some point.

Bonus Tip: Giving discounts is a strategic choice every business or salesperson needs a philosophy for. If you are open to giving discounts, be sure there's a reason for doing so. Giving a discount because you're not comfortable charging your prices is not a good enough reason. When offering a discount that the client specifically requested, ask for something in return. This builds value for both the client and yourself. It creates a win/win relationship. Beware of offering discounts that only benefit one party. Chances are you or your client will end up regretting the deal, and this may damage the relationship long-term.

5. Stay Away from Fear-Based Selling

To help you create the perfect proposals, step away from creating fear for your potential client.

Fear doesn't work for everyone, and it's so overused at this point that a lot of people tune it out. Those who keep an eye out for fear-based selling—and actively avoid it—may also be avoiding you if this is your approach to sales. In my opinion, the reward isn't worth the risk.

Don't pitch using fear.

We are bombarded every day with negativity. Scroll through your newsfeed on Facebook, and you'll probably see someone encouraging others to post funny videos, photos of kids, or anything to lighten the mood.

A few weeks back, I found myself in the audience as someone got up to talk about her company and products. The whole presentation was based in fear. She listed all the harmful chemicals other companies use in their products, all the ways people damage themselves when using those products, and on and on it went. It was the blue zebra by a factor of ten. By the time she was done, everyone in the audience, like me, probably had a crystal-clear image of a product that was exactly the opposite of hers.

Please understand, this woman is a kind and smart business professional. She did what her company taught her to do: use fear to motivate people into buying her products. However, she was missing some crucial information in her presentation. She was missing the joy, the benefits, and the positivity behind her products. As much as I like this woman, I found myself completely shutting down during her talk. In the end, I had zero interest in learning more because I operate under the premise of "Consumer Protection for My Own Mind."

Like many people out there, the fear-based approach doesn't hold my interest. This doesn't mean I take a Pollyanna approach to all areas of my life. It does mean fear is not a motivator for me to spend my hard-earned dollars.

Now, here's the kicker: her product was something most people found joy in using. The audience would have naturally responded much better to how awesome it was over the "don't do" and "shouldn't use" statements she made.

Please keep in mind; I'm not implying that you shouldn't be sharing the cons whenever you pitch to a potential client. Instead, I'm suggesting you include the positives within your pitch as well. There needs to be balance in your sales approach. A few people will be attracted to the fear-based selling. However, many won't. The idea of adding a balance of positive and some negative (when appropriate) will strengthen the way you create rapport through your presentation, and by extension, broaden your potential client base.

6. Change Up Your Proposal Verbiage

Albert Einstein said, "The definition of insanity is doing something over and over again and expecting a different result."

Too often, I encounter people who, instead of tailoring their presentation to each client, stick with the same canned message for everyone. When you do this, you come across as salesy. Most of us don't want to be "sold." We want authentic connection with real conversation.

Recently, a man reached out wanting to sell me his services. His main selling technique was name-dropping. This is where the salesperson throws out names of people they know or have done business with to build credibility.

The technique can be effective when used strategically. However, in our conversation, the names he dropped were unfamiliar to me. Every time he would ask if I knew *so and so*, I would tell him *no*. He would act shocked at my lack of knowledge of these *big name* people. After about five name-drop fails, I expected him to try a new approach. Nope. He was committed to the name-drop technique. After about twelve names, it became comical. I started to giggle every time he threw out a new name.

This went on for about fifteen minutes. By the time he was up to twenty names, I was incredulous. He was so committed to his one sales technique that he refused to accept it was doing him more harm than good.

At one point, I stopped him and said, "I understand your approach, but name-dropping is not an effective way to influence me. It will not earn my business." He acknowledged that he heard me and then within a minute dropped another name. I ended the call.

The lesson? When your approach with a client isn't working, do something else.

One of my favorite sayings is, "Blessed are the flexible, for they shall not be bent out of shape." You must be flexible and tailor your proposal to what's most interesting to each client.

1. This means you've got to:
2. Know your product/service inside out,
3. Be prepared to uncover and overcome objections, and
4. Pay complete attention to the client.

When you do these things, it's much easier to have a conversation with the client and not stress about the pitch. You can still keep the sale front-of-mind while being authentic.

It's also easier to pivot in a new direction. Canned presentations make people sound inexperienced. Sticking to an ineffective sales technique gives the impression of being unaware of social cues.

If you are like many of my clients, you will enjoy sales conversations much more with this approach. More importantly, your client will enjoy engaging with you at a deeper level.

7. Use Words That Motivate and Influence

Do you have trigger words?

Words that pique your interest or even stop you in your tracks when you hear them?

Most of us have a few trigger words. One of the biggest challenges is knowing the right words to use with a prospect/client to move them to action.

You can't ask a prospect, "What words should I use to earn your business?" When you know how to pay attention, huge clues will appear in the types of words they're using. I like to think of these as big flashing neon signs saying, "This is how to motivate and influence me."

One of the best times to pick up on a client's preferred words is when they answer your questions. For instance, when you ask a client, "What's important to you when choosing . . . (insert your product/service here)?" their language will depict one of three styles:

1. They focus on what they want to happen—toward language.
2. They focus on what they don't want to happen—away-from language.
3. They focus on a mix of what they want and what they don't want—a mix of toward and away-from language.

Please note, one style is not better than another. This is simply information that creates a more effective conversation with a prospect or client.

As an example, I generally ask prospects, "What's important to you right now concerning your selling skills?"

Responses might come in the form of:

1. **Toward Language:** "I want to feel more confident and know what to say when talking about my products/services." The focus is on what they want to have happen.
2. **Away-From Language:** "I struggle with the idea of asking people for money, and I don't want to come off as being salesy." The focus is on what they don't want to happen.
3. **The Mix:** "I want to feel confident when asking for business, and I don't want to come off as being salesy." The focus is a mix of what they want and don't want.

By picking up these types of clues, you'll have a better understanding of how to deliver a proposal to the client. Here are some examples of how to respond when proposing to work together:

1. **Toward Language:** "The outcome of our work together will include giving you a renewed sense of confidence and new key phrases for sales conversations." The focus is on what they gain as a result of our working together.

2. **Away-From Language:** "After working together, you'll no longer worry about money-related conversations or fear coming across salesy when inviting people to work with you." The focus is on ensuring what they fear will not happen after we work together.

3. **Mix:** "As a result of our working together, your confidence will grow from honing your selling skills, and you'll no longer have to worry about sounding unprofessional in client conversations." The focus is on getting them some of what they want and saving them from what they don't want.

Once you have an understanding of your prospect or client's preferred language, you'll be better able to deliver information in a way they are more open to receiving it. This will not only increase the success rate of your pitch; it will build rapport as well.

Now, it's your turn. Draft up to three of your top recommendations in the workbook space below. These should be offers that will meet most of your clients' needs since you are drafting them without client information.

_____

_____

_____

Remember, when you engage with clients, reexamine these offers, and adjust them before presenting. You might even need to switch one of these options out for another offer that is a better fit for that prospective client.

Top-Down Selling

Relax your hands, and hold them out in front of you, palms facing up. Notice how your fingers tend to curl in.

We come out of the womb already knowing how to grasp things. It's no surprise that, as adults, we love to make attachments to material goods. Because of this, when delivering a proposal, start with the most expensive of your three options, and work your way down. This is known as top-down selling.

As humans, we don't like to have things taken away. Top-down selling allows you to focus on what a prospect must give up in order to have a lower price. Now, if you had started at the least expensive option and tried to work your way up, the potential client would feel as if you were trying to upsell them.

Remember, when crafting your proposal, you must start with the best option that *fits the client's needs*. You might have a $20,000 package. However, if your $5,000 package is a better fit for your client, you shouldn't recommend the $20,000 package. You'd be selling them something they don't need, which would hurt your integrity and ultimately cause distrust with your client. Start with the $5,000 package. You'll be giving the client the best solution for their need without putting your credibility at risk.

Your proposal should also make the decision easy for your client. Remove all language and options that will hinder their decision-making process. Doing so will increase your conversions during closing and lead to healthier professional relationships.

CHAPTER 5
Step 5: Close

Being proficient at closing sales is one of the most requested skills I'm asked to teach. You can have the best product or service at the best price and still struggle to make money if you don't know how to close.

Like most things, there's a structure to the closing process. Understanding this will make closing easier.

Three Steps to Closing

1. Lead the closing process. First, remember, you're the expert. It's your job to take the lead in the closing process. Business owners who wait for the prospect to take the lead will likely wind up with no sale at all.

2. Ask for the sale. Once you've given pricing or provided a proposal, you must *ask* for the sale.

3. Wait. Don't say a word after you ask for the sale until your prospect responds. At this step, there is some critical language that makes it easy for the prospect to make a decision on your proposal. Salespeople who keep talking after they've issued the closing language will likely talk themselves out of the sale (more on this later in the chapter). So, with lots of care and kindness, I'm telling you to zip it. You'll know how to proceed once the prospect responds.

Closing Language

As with most aspects of this process, there is a strategy behind closing language. Here is a prime example, delivered after the proposal: "After reviewing these options, which feels like the best fit for you right now?"

It is important that you craft your closing in a way that lets you deliver it, then be silent. I can't stress this enough.

If you speak before they respond, you are now selling past the close. (If you want a tip to avoid selling past the close, please check out my book *Six Word Lessons on Influencing with Grace.*[5]) You might confuse the client and talk them out of working with you. Be willing to let them take whatever time they need to process. Many people struggle with being quiet. Silence is an advanced sales technique and worth mastering. It will serve you in many situations.

Now let's take a quick look at the line I used. "After reviewing these options, which feels like the best fit for you right now?" There is an embedded command in that language that says, in a really nice way, *make a decision.* The command is the phrase, "right now."

The reason for this is to combat decision fatigue. Many of us like it when people help us make decisions. Life bombards us with decisions all day long. So, when you say to your client or prospect, "After reviewing these options, which feels like the best fit for you right now?" you're making it easy for them to take some time, think about it, and give you a response. This is crucial to your success.

Seems pretty simple, doesn't it? Using these three steps to close, with the right language, can make magic happen. Of course, it doesn't always happen this way.

Troubleshooting the Closing Process

Let's discuss a few situations that may pop up in the closing process and what can be done about them.

I Need to Think About It

You've invited a prospect to work with you, and they've said, "I need to think about it." What do you do next?

---

5   Check out www.yoursalesmaven.com/the-book to get your copy!

First, check that you've covered everything they need in order to think over your invitation. Ask them, "Is there any additional information that I might provide to help you make a good decision?"

Tread carefully here. Your job is not to go into convincing mode. If you do, you will often convince people not to hire you. Nobody likes to be coerced. Convincing mode signals a hard sales push when, in fact, they need time to think about it. Please be very respectful in those moments.

Here is some circle-back language to use after you've checked in about additional information: "Take the time that you need to think about it. About how much time do you think you'll need?"

Pause. Wait. See what they say.

Then say, "Let's go ahead and get a circle-back call scheduled now. That way, we can discuss any additional questions that come to mind, and we can decide at that point the best next steps." Suggest a day or time within the next week, and get it on their calendar so they don't get swamped by other commitments. That way, when somebody says, "I want to think about it," you don't just say, "Great! Let me know."

Not everyone will agree to schedule the circle-back call. However, willingness to schedule that call is a strong indicator that the prospect *is* going to think about it. I would advise keeping your circle-back calls to thirty minutes. Time is money.

It's your job to make moving through the process easy for the client. That means you have to offer the circle-back call every single time.

When you get on the circle-back call, go into it with the intention of working toward the next step. Then, be willing to just have a conversation. Check to see what questions come up, address those questions, and then issue another invitation.

Circle-Back Call Example

I had a really great circle-back call with a woman who was very interested in my proposal. She wanted to talk to her husband first, however.

Here's the language I used after she asked if she could take some time to think about it: "Yes, please do. Have a conversation with your husband. Take the time you need to think about it. About how much time do you think you'll need? Let's go ahead and schedule a circle-back call."

When we got on our scheduled circle-back call, I could hear in her voice that she was probably going to say *no*, but it's not my job to make an assumption about that. It's my job to do everything I can on that circle-back call to make it easy for her to work with me.

Even though my brain was screaming, "Nikki, she's gonna say *no*," I still moved forward with the process and asked, "Did you have a chance to talk with your husband? How did that go? What questions have come to mind since we last spoke?"

She said, "You know, we talked about it, and he's not opposed to it. It's just that it's a lot of money up front for us. Money's tight right now."

"I totally understand," I said. "That makes sense. You need to make a decision that makes sense for your family and also for your business. If I was able to offer you a payment plan, is that something you'd be interested in?"

"Well," she said, "I'm not really sure."

She hemmed and hawed. Notice that I didn't launch into saying, "Well if it's money, we could talk about payment plans. Here are my payment plans!" First, I got permission to see if she was even interested. There's no point in wasting my breath talking about payment plans if it's something she's not even interested in hearing about.

She finally said, "Okay Nikki. Tell me about your payment plans."

After I walked her through the payment plan, she said, "You know what? I can tell I just need to work with you. I want to be able to do exactly what you did by getting my client on the call, walking them through this, allowing them to have the time and the space that they need to make the decision."

Then she paid me in full.

Even though we talked about payment plans, because I was willing to give her the time she needed to circle back, she became a paying client, and I closed the sale.

My philosophy as far as the sales process goes is that I will stay in it as long as the client stays in it with me. As soon as they ask me to jump through a bunch of hoops or blow off my calls or don't respond, I stop. At that point, the ball is in their court because I don't chase clients in order to close the sale. If we start chasing clients, they act like toddlers! If you say to a toddler, "I'm going to chase you!" they run!

Be willing to let them go away, and also be willing to keep engaging with them if they need further circle-backs.

The Long Close

Some people are going to buy from you the first time you talk, and others are going to take a while. One of my VIP clients had me on her list to hire for three years before she became a VIP client.

Now, I didn't actually know this until she reached out to me, yet in her mind, I had to do a lot of things to earn her business. Remember when I talked about your convincer strategy in Chapter Two? My platform helped her stay engaged with me (my newsletter of weekly sales tips, social media posts, and more), so when she was ready, it was easy for her to become a VIP client.

Sometimes, second or third circle-back calls happen with clients. On your first call, maybe they need more time to check into a possible blocker to doing business with you. As long as you are offering to do another circle-back call, and they are saying *yes*, they're still in it. I would be open to three or four circle-back calls as long as the client and I were moving through the process, and they were keeping with their commitments.

Be sure, however, when you feel every question has been answered, that you ask for the prospect's business. You might have issued invitations and not received solid answers. In cases like this, where the two of you have entered into a circle-back loop, you must be more direct in your invitation to do business. Be sure to first put the prospect at ease, deepen rapport, then ask, "What will it take to earn your business?"

This question requires a concrete answer from the client. After asking this, you should receive a list of what the client requires so that you can get out of the loop and on to doing business with them.

There will be times when a prospect is interested, but they cannot commit to circling back within a definite time frame. In those cases, the language I use is: "Hey, I would love to earn your business when you're ready, so please reach out to me when I can be of service to you."

Throwing the ball back in their court doesn't mean that I don't want to work with them. I'm just moving on to prospects interested now. When they come back later (which happens all the time), I will be thrilled and honored to work with them.

Receiving "No"

No can be hard to hear. Yet you must know what to say in order to maintain rapport with the prospect even when they say *no*. Sometimes, a *no* is just a *not now*. Be willing to set aside disappointment, and focus on keeping the relationship intact. People often come back when they're ready to buy. However, they absolutely will not return if you leave the conversation poorly.

A while ago, I was contacted by a woman wanting to sell me her products. When she invited me to do business with her, I declined. She then offered to send me some information via email. I agreed to look it over. A week later she asked to schedule a call with me. She didn't indicate what she wanted to chat about, and I was under the impression she was interested in hiring me for some work with her team based on a previous discussion we'd had.

When we got on the phone, she wanted to know if I had gone through the information she'd sent me. I explained I hadn't received an email from her and had not looked any further at her products. While on the phone with me, she realized she'd sent the email to the wrong person and then proceeded to walk me through multiple pages of a website to lead to a product page where she asked me to place an order.

I felt a little overwhelmed by having to jump through so many hoops while on the phone with her. I told her in a kind way, "I appreciate you taking the time to share more information with me about your product. To be honest, I'm feeling overwhelmed, and I'm not interested in placing an order."

Her whole demeanor changed after that, and I could tell she was upset with me.

Her response: "Nikki, you said you were willing to try my product, and now you're saying you're not willing."

I said, "I'm so sorry if I gave you that impression. I thought I had agreed to look over an email you were going to send, which I didn't receive. And now, looking at your website, I know this product is not a good fit for me."

Her next response, "Hmm, well . . . ok then. I guess I'll just see you around." Then she hung up.

It was awkward. I felt irritated and bad at the same time. I liked this woman, even though her product was not for me. Given the interaction, however, I knew that, should I have need of that product, I would be seeking out other vendors.

How you respond to the client after they decline can make or break your opportunity to do business with them in the future. A prospect's situation might change. What doesn't change is a bad impression.

Here is some language to use when you receive a *no*. "Thank you for the time you've given me. I'd sure appreciate the chance to earn your business in the future if/when you may need my product/ service."

After delivering a reply like this, spend a few minutes chatting with the client. It can be about anything. Send the non-verbal message that your relationship is still important. Leave the meeting with the client feeling good about the interaction. They are more likely to come back to you in the future when they do need your services or product.

CHAPTER 6
Tips to Move Your Clients Through the Selling Staircase

Now that we've reviewed the Selling Staircase from start to finish, let's discuss a few things that will help you take your client from one step to another.

Remember, when people don't buy from you, they're missing out on how you can fulfill their greatest need. This is all about showing people that you hear them, understand them, and are willing to do what it takes to earn their business.

To get you started, here are a few quick, practical tips to move you and your client through the staircase.

1. It's not about you. Relationship selling is not about you. Your focus needs to be finding out what the client needs. When you can set aside all your internal dialogue and completely focus on the prospect, making the sale will get so much easier. The relationship comes before the sale!

2. Don't convince. I'm a firm believer that you cannot convince people to buy from you. We don't want to be convinced!

3. Be yourself. Sometimes clients are worried initially that a structure like the Selling Staircase makes the sales process too rigid. In my experience, I've found that once you understand the structure of the Selling Staircase, it allows your personality to shine through. Being your authentic self does work.

4. Issue invitations at every step. I know I've said this before, and the point bears repeating here: You must issue an invitation. This is the number one way to increase sales. If you don't ask prospects to move to the next step, they're not going to move. When you don't issue invitations, you also leave people unsatisfied.

Caring, Not Assuming

Recently a client expressed some frustration over a situation where a prospective customer scheduled a phone appointment and then didn't answer at the scheduled time. My client left a voicemail and sent a follow-up email checking in about rescheduling the appointment. Days later, she hadn't heard anything back from the customer.

Has this ever happened to you?

It can be difficult to move through the Selling Staircase when you have a client who expressed interest in your product/service, then dropped off the face of the earth. Do you assume they're no longer interested? How many times do you follow up before you make the decision to move on?

After digging a little deeper into the communication between my client and her prospective customer, it was apparent the interest level was high initially. She wasn't sure why her prospect had lost interest or what to do next.

My recommendation to her, "Don't assume your customer has lost interest. We don't have enough information yet to determine what's happened. Let's approach her from a place of authentic concern to ensure she's ok and see if there's anything she needs."

With that in mind, I outlined specific language for her to use on her next follow-up call to the prospective customer.

After listening to the follow-up message, the prospective customer called right back to say that she was dealing with a family tragedy and was still interested in working together. One week later, she became a paying customer.

Caring is key to relationship selling. Follow up with clients when they miss appointments with genuine concern for their well-being. Check in to make sure they are ok.

Here's a possible way to phrase a follow-up call in this scenario:

"Hello Sally, this is Nikki Rausch from Sales Maven. I wanted to check in and make sure you are ok. I'm concerned as you missed our scheduled appointment, and I haven't heard from you. Is there anything you need? Please let me know all is well with you. We can easily reschedule your appointment. You can reach me at [NUMBER]. Take care, Sally; I'm sending good thoughts your way."

If you received a voicemail like this, would you be inclined to return the call to put the person's mind at ease? Especially if something did actually go wrong, wouldn't it be nice to know someone noticed and was willing to check in with you?

The most successful salespeople I know care about their clients. The relationship should come before the sale.

Safely Using Intensity

As you are noticing the trends in this book, you have likely realized that relationship selling (what I teach) is about developing rapport.

It's about taking the time to understand the client's needs and then delivering a solution to meet those needs. It's my belief that when you make the relationship the priority, the selling process flows naturally. The "old way" of selling is a lot more aggressive than that, and not something I often recommend.

The time to bring intensity to the selling process is into deciding what you want to accomplish before the meeting, and in keeping it front-of-mind throughout.

Too often, people start client meetings without having put any thought into the desired outcome. When you go into a meeting without an outcome in mind, it's the equivalent of starting a road trip from Washington state to New York without a GPS. There's a good chance there'll be some wrong turns, and it will probably take you much longer to get there than if you used the GPS on your phone/in your car to start.

Before each meeting, you should know what the logical next step is and what needs to happen in the meeting to get you and the client to the next step (perhaps up the staircase). It's moving through the step-by-step approach where you exchange dollars for services.

Without an outcome in mind, people often end client meetings without having the next step scheduled. Big mistake. HUGE!

You have heard me say this before—telling a client you'll send them a proposal is not enough. Set a date to review the proposal. This means a date and time scheduled on both of your calendars. Without the date and time set, you're likely to never get the client on the phone again. You'll spend useless time and energy wondering if/when you'll hear from the client. You slow down the process when you don't have the next step scheduled.

Being intentional (and even a little intense) about keeping the process moving is crucial to both you and your client getting needs met. However, this intensity should not take away from the rapport and the relationship building you do in your client meetings.

Having an outcome in mind also applies to networking events.

For example, when attending a networking meeting, I spend five to ten minutes setting up my outcome. A technique I created and teach my clients is what I call the 3, 2, 1 of Networking

3: Meet 3 new people

2: Deepen rapport with 2 people in the room that I already have a relationship with.

1: Book 1 follow-up appointment, which means getting something on a prospect's calendar as well as mine.

At the end of the networking meeting, I have a way to measure my success. How did I do in relation to my outcome? What should I do differently next time?

Bonus Tip: The 3, 2, 1 of Networking tip is something I often use when I attend a conference or any business event. It doesn't matter if there are 30 people in the room or 3,000. It's about making real connections. If you can meet more than three people and have a real connection, that's just a bonus.

Keeping the Process Moving

When you're moving a client through the Selling Staircase and ultimately towards exchanging money for services/product, it's important to never end a conversation with a prospective client without attempting to schedule the next step.

Sometimes you can move a client through all the steps in one conversation. However, it often takes multiple interactions before you get to the top of the Selling Staircase. Therefore, it's your job to seamlessly move a client through the process. If you're leaving conversations and not scheduling the next talk, you're going to expend a ton of energy and time trying to get that person on the phone again.

Too often clients tell me about amazing meetings they had with potential clients and then when I ask about the next scheduled appointment, they say, "Oh, I just figured I'd call them next week and take it from there."

Now let me ask you something: when your phone rings, and you're not expecting the call, do you answer?

I often ask this question when I'm delivering my signature talk at speaking gigs. The people in the audience are asked to raise their hands if they answer unexpected phone calls. Usually, less than 10% of the people in the room raise their hands.

So, when you don't get your next appointment on the prospect's calendar, you significantly diminish your chances of ever closing that sale. People get busy, they get distracted, or sometimes they buy from your competitor because it's convenient. All that hard work you put into earning the person's time and attention is now wasted because you missed this key step.

Don't forget to take your cues from the prospect, however. When you offer to schedule the next step, and they respond with, "Don't call me, I'll call you," respect their request. My suggestion in these instances is that you reply with, "Great. I'd love to earn your business. Please reach out at any point with questions and/or when you're ready to take the next step. I'll be excited to hear from you."

Now that you know the intricacies of the Selling Staircase, and have some tips for moving through it, I want to talk about building rapport—which is crucial to this whole process.

CHAPTER 7
Building Rapport

Rapport is paramount.

It is foundational. It is critical. If it falls apart—the whole stairway may crumble. Without rapport, you have nothing because people buy from those they know, like, and trust. When you have a foundation of rapport, it gets so much easier to move your client through the steps. Most clients will give you some grace, even when things get bumpy, because they already feel comfortable with you.

Salesy Salespeople

Have you ever met someone and instantly thought to yourself, "this person is only interested in selling me something?"

Often when I give a keynote presentation, I ask the audience to describe the behaviors of someone who's *salesy*. I almost always get the response, "They are more interested in what they want than in what I need."

If you're like me, that is an instant turnoff. Too many people are approaching sales as if the only thing that matters is closing the sale. This type of thinking manifests itself in the form of desperate, pushy, and aggressive behaviors. These behaviors do way more damage to your client relationships than you can imagine.

Too many people forget the client must come first if you want to sustain a long-term, successful working relationship.

The first step in building a relationship is establishing rapport. Without rapport, it doesn't matter if you have the best product, best price, or even if you're the only game in town—people will look for another solution. In today's evolving marketplace, someone will offer an alternative solution, and better customer service as well.

Ways to Invest in Rapport

When I first meet someone, I imagine opening up a rapport bank account. When I do a good job, I make a deposit in that account. And when I make a mistake, I withdraw against that account. The goal is to make a deposit each time I come into contact with this person—building up balances with everyone I meet.

When you build up enough credits with people, all kinds of great things happen. And it can happen quickly. Your rapport account can get full the first time you meet somebody. Often, though, it takes a little bit of time.

Do you have a favorite restaurant? A place you've frequented more than twenty times? Every time you've eaten there, you've had amazing service and well-prepared food. Now, imagine you go there this weekend, and your food comes out lukewarm. You've had so many great experiences at the restaurant that you're likely willing to give them the benefit of the doubt and go back.

However, imagine you go to a restaurant for the first time, and the food comes out cold. Are you more likely or less likely to give them a second chance? More than likely, you're not going to eat there again. This new place doesn't have any deposits in their rapport back account.

Think of how you build rapport with your clients. Maybe you make it easy for them to connect with you. Maybe you seek them out or even send a little note. Maybe you see them at a networking event and greet them without asking for anything in return. That is how you make deposits into the rapport account. You want to be sure you have a sufficient balance for that one time you make a misstep and end up making a withdrawal.

Now, it's your turn. What can you do to build rapport with the people you encounter?

For many people, this is an easy list to create. Yet when I ask clients if they do any of the things on the list, they give me a blank stare. It has never crossed their minds to go above and beyond to make people feel valued and appreciated! And you should appreciate all of your clients.

_____

_____

_____

_____

Let's go a little deeper. Below are not only ways to avoid having to make a withdrawal, but also great rapport-building behaviors to help you increase those account balances!

Permission Before the Pitch

A surefire way to ruin a relationship is by misleading someone. Whether you fib to your partner, your boss, your best friend, or to your client, the relationship will suffer and may even be damaged beyond repair.

Have you ever had someone ask to discuss an agreed upon topic only to spend the whole meeting *selling* you on their product/service?

This is known as the "Bait and Switch."

Launching into a pitch without taking the time to get permission, build rapport, and show respect to your client is rarely an effective selling technique. This is a common misstep in many of the networking groups I participate in. I wish there weren't so many examples to choose from (my clients have shared many with me). I will include one of my own examples of receiving the bait and switch.

A while back, a woman contacted me through my business Facebook page and asked if we could schedule a time to chat about how I might help her with her sales. We had previously met at a networking group luncheon.

When we got on the phone, and I asked her to share a little about her business and how I might help her, she launched into a sales pitch for her product. When I asked her again what she had in mind with regards to us working together, she said she thought her product would be a good fit for my business.

In the end, she wanted to sell to me, and in order to get me on the phone, she misled me by acting as if she was interested in becoming a client. Needless to say, I felt lied to, and her lack of integrity was a complete turnoff. She had zero chance of getting my business, and I certainly would not recommend her or her product to anyone I know.

I have no idea if this is how companies are advising their sales-people to book appointments or get conversations going. However, as you can see, it's not working. When someone's first impression is, "you're a lovely person," and her next impression is, "I'll be making an effort to keep my distance," you've ruined your reputation and damaged the relationship.

What to do?

Be transparent regarding your intentions when setting up a meeting with a prospective client.

Your integrity and honesty will be appreciated. And if your honesty means a person declines to meet with you, then you've saved yourself time and effort to focus on clients in need of your product/ service. To be clear, you can bring up your business/product/service during a meeting when appropriate. Wait for the right time, and do it with respect for the other person/people in the meeting.

Here's a possible language suggestion on broaching the topic of your business during a meeting:

I know the purpose of the meeting is to discuss XYZ, and I'm looking forward to it. As you may or may not know, one of the services I offer for my VIP clients is to edit their client emails. Knowing you communicate with your clients quite often over email, this might be something you'd benefit from. If you're interested in learning more, I'd be happy to chat with you at the end of our meeting or set up another time to discuss it. Let me know if that's something you'd like more information on.

Then you wait and see what the other person says. If they say they're interested, then you wait until the end of your meeting, or you set up a time to chat about it. If they say they'll let you know, then turn the discussion back to the original topic of the meeting. You might follow up a few days later and check to see if they'd like to schedule a time to discuss the product/service you offered.

When you get permission first to talk about your product/service, prospects will be much more open to listening and considering your offer.

Plus, you keep the rapport intact and your reputation solid.

Apologize and Correct

Not too long ago, my guy and I went to a local restaurant for dinner. This was a place we frequented about once a month. On this particular occasion, the waitress was not attentive, forgot to bring our appetizer, didn't refill our drinks, and brought out something we didn't even order. Then she disappeared without checking on us. By the time she came back to bring us our bill, we were frustrated. I kindly pointed out that she'd made a few missteps with our order, and her response was, "My bad. I'll do better next time."

What's interesting is this response of *my bad* seems to be commonly used in place of an apology.

Since this incident at the restaurant, I've heard more and more people saying it. Giving a reply like this in place of "I'm sorry" comes across as dismissive and further exacerbates the problem.

What to do? When something goes amiss with a customer,

apologize and then do what you can to correct the situation. When apologizing, actually say the words. "I apologize for (fill in the issue); please forgive me. Let me see what I can do to make this right." Then move on to finding a solution.

You don't have to beat yourself up or fall at your customer's feet when mistakes are made, yet a real apology will go so much further than a flippant response like, "My bad." It's always a good idea to put yourself in your customer's shoes, think about how you'd want to be treated, and then respond accordingly.

Requests for Patience

How would you feel if someone forced you to endure a situation you did not want . . . and then thanked you for it? I'm guessing not great. The truth is, you might be doing this all the time and not realizing it.

When something goes wrong, and a client brings it to your attention, do you thank them for "being patient" while you attempt to make things right? Did the client agree to be patient in the first place? If not, then why are you thanking them for something you're essentially forcing on them?

It's common to thank people for being patient; however, is it having the effect you want and (more importantly) helping your rapport? When you're in the position of being the client, would you rather be respectfully asked if you're willing to be patient or have the person assume you will be?

What to do? Avoid thanking clients for their patience when it's not being freely given. When things are not going well, consider asking if the client is willing to be patient while you come up with a solution. Remember, these situations are opportunities to deepen the level of rapport when done thoughtfully.

Most people send emails or say to clients things like:

1. Thank you for your patience while I research this situation and get back to you.
2. Thank you for your patience. I'll get back to you once I have some more information.
3. Thank you for your patience while I find a solution.

These phrases may read ok to you. To an upset client, however, they may come off as flippant or even condescending. The last thing you want to do is escalate a situation and lose a client.

Here are a few possible ways you might rephrase your requests:

1. Thank you for bringing this situation to my attention. Would you be willing to give me a little bit of time to research this and get back to you?
2. Please forgive me for this misstep. I apologize. With your permission, I'd like to take a little bit of time to come up with a few possible solutions and get back to you later today. Would that be acceptable?
3. I apologize for dropping the ball. Would you be open to giving me another chance to make this right between us? With your permission, let's set up a time in the next few days to get on the phone and talk about how best I can resolve this situation to your satisfaction.

Asking clients for permission is much more effective than assuming you have it and bulldozing over them.

Be Vulnerable

There's a lot of talk about the power of vulnerability and how it connects people.

Since a big part of what I teach is building rapport and developing long-term client relationships, the concept of vulnerability comes up frequently.

At one of my speaking events, a therapist in the audience bravely approached me after my talk to challenge me on a tip I shared about leaving off disclaimers when meeting someone for the first time. (The reason to leave off disclaimers is that it diminishes your credibility with potential clients.) A few common disclaimers are saying things like, "I'm nervous," or "I'm a mess," or "I wish I felt more prepared . . ." Disclaimers tend to come from your negative self-talk or internal critic.

She wanted to know what my thoughts were on the difference between sharing vulnerable moments with clients and making a disclaimer. Her clients often feel nervous on their first visit with her, and she wants to relate to them in order to put them at ease.

Sharing a personal story or struggle with the intent of connecting on a deeper level is appropriate. This is what I consider being vulnerable.

Disclaimers tend to be something we say because we're feeling insecure.

The example I shared with her was to imagine having a new patient come in to work with her and telling the patient she was nervous and hoping she did a good job (disclaimer). That patient is there paying good money for her expertise and expects a high level of service. Sharing a story about a time in her life when she was doing something for the first time and feeling nervous or anxious about it (vulnerability), on the other hand, is a way to relate to the patient.

Unfortunately, too many people have confused the when and how to be vulnerable and are turning clients off.

Not too long ago, I witnessed a woman sharing her personal story to be vulnerable to potential clients. Her story started with her at a very young age and chronicled every bad thing that had ever happened in her life. It took her more than twenty minutes to share her story. Instead of feeling like she connected with the people in attendance, it felt more like a therapy session. The participants were the therapists, and she'd become the patient. By the time she finished, the room just sat there, stunned. Nobody had a response, no one asked any questions, and most of us took the opportunity to leave the room. It was awkward and uncomfortable for all involved.

Now had she shared just one of her experiences and related it back to the people in the room, that would have been a more appropriate vulnerable moment.

Giving out a laundry list of everything that's ever happened to you isn't about the connection between you and the other person. It's making the conversation all about you. In sales, and in building relationships, that's not an effective way to go.

What to do? Share a personal struggle as a means to connect yourself with another person. Avoid overwhelming people with too much story. Before sharing a vulnerable moment, be clear as to the purpose. Do you want to connect with someone, or do you want people to feel empathy for you?

Of course, there is nothing wrong with wanting empathy. However, there is a time and place for it. When building relationships with clients, share vulnerable moments as a way to relate and engage with the other person.

Get in Sync

A simple way to build and deepen rapport with clients is to get in sync with their speech patterns. Doing this takes less energy for you, and they pay heightened attention, converse better, and ask more questions.

A few reasons you want to get in sync and maintain rapport are because it:

- Increases your likability
- Builds trust
- Establishes your credibility

- Makes it easier for clients to say *yes*, and
- Encourages clients to be more revealing about how to earn their business

Notice your client's rate of speech. Is it significantly faster or slower than your normal rate of speech? Be willing to either speed up or slow down depending on the client. This will put them at ease because it sets your conversations at a speed they are comfortable with.

Think about the last time you were in a conversation with someone who had a significantly different rate of speech than you. Was it uncomfortable? When you're a fast talker and are speaking with someone slower than you, conversing with them can be like swimming through molasses.

If you have a slower rate of speech and find yourself in conversation with someone who speaks faster than you, it can be aggravating when they talk over you or finish your sentences.

You want to make conversations as comfortable as possible for clients to stay engaged. Adding flexibility to your own behavior so you're in sync with your client is a quick and easy way to build and maintain rapport.

Bonus Tip: If you want to end a conversation, change up your rate of speech to be the opposite of the other person's. Chances are they'll wrap up their conversation much quicker to get out of the uncomfortable difference in your rates of speech.

Pace and Lead

Once, while I was doing a corporate sales training, one of the attendees shared how difficult it was to work with and sell to people in certain occupations. He said, "They're so serious and hard to interact with that I find myself cracking jokes and doing everything I can to lighten the mood."

He wanted to know if there was a technique or skill he could apply to be more effective because cracking jokes didn't seem to work in his favor. To be effective in sales, it's your job to put your client at ease. It's unrealistic to expect your client to match your behavior by doing the exact opposite of what they normally do.

Remember, it is not about you; it's about them.

Be flexible in your behavior and take what I call the "pace and lead" approach.

For example, in the scenario listed above, a much more effective strategy is to match the other person's behavior. Start out being more serious (pace), then, when appropriate, try lightening the mood by adding a light-hearted comment, and see how your client reacts (lead). If your client laughs, lightens up, or changes their behavior, you can continue to lead. If your client maintains their serious behavior, your best bet is to continue to match (pace) your client.

It boils down to this simple decision; do you want to earn business with clients who have different styles than yours? If so, pacing is an important step in building rapport and putting the client at ease.

Creating Safe Environments for Building Rapport

An important selling technique is knowing how to create a safe environment for your clients. Safety can come in many forms and serve multiple purposes in the selling process. Safety in the context I'm talking about is knowing how to put your clients at ease so they're open to hearing your message and doing business with you.

One of the biggest mistakes salespeople make is poorly communicating expectations. This makes the client unsure of what to do next, leading to a breakdown in rapport that might cost you the sale.

Here's an example from my own experience:

A while back, I sat down with a woman to find out more about her product. She talked for fifteen minutes about the product and then said, "So do you want to sign up to be a customer?"

I didn't really know what to say. I wasn't sure what signing up to be a customer meant as she hadn't covered it in her presentation. I politely declined, and we ended the meeting. I walked away feeling confused and, frankly, a little disappointed in her selling skills. It wasn't that I didn't want her product; it was the uncertainty about what I was supposed to do next that stopped me. Since she didn't create an environment where I felt safe to ask questions, I ended up buying the product from someone else.

When I sat down with another representative from the same company, the new rep told me up front what we'd cover in our session (pre-framing). She encouraged me to ask questions and let me know that at the end of the meeting she'd explain the different levels of being a customer. She also covered how to get set up as a customer and how to place my first order.

She created a safe environment. I knew what to expect during our time together, and it was clear how to take the next step to become a customer. I was able to ask questions, and she was a valuable resource in the process. Same company, same product; the difference was the sales approach.

You've probably heard in a presentation training course that you should, "Tell your client what you're going to tell them; tell them; then tell them what you told them," right? Well, good news! This is also an excellent way to create safety with a client. Let clients know what to expect, give them what they expected, and then clarify that their expectations were met.

One way to ensure that your client's expectations were met is by asking. A favorite question of mine is to ask a client toward the end of our meeting: "What (if anything) hasn't been covered yet that you'd like more information on?" This gives the client the opportunity to ask any last questions. Once they acknowledge that their expectations were met, I set up our next meeting to keep them moving through the selling process.

Now, it's your turn. Create a safe selling environment by letting your client know what to expect at the start of a meeting.

_____

_____

_____

_____

_____

Specificity Counts

A common theme among my clients is frustration over a lack of response from potential customers. Once we dig into their communications (phone and email messaging), it's clear—they're too vague.

The answer? Be more specific, and you'll make it easier for clients to say, "Yes!"

Here are two examples. Which do you think is more effective?

Example 1: A prospective client calls and leaves you a message stating they want to set up an appointment with you. When you call them back, you get their voicemail. You leave a message saying how much you're looking forward to working with them and leave your number, asking them to call you back at their convenience to get an appointment scheduled.

Example 2: A prospective client calls and leaves you a message stating they want to set up an appointment with you. When you call them back, you get their voicemail. You leave a message saying how much you are looking forward to working with them and that you have time available Monday at 10:00 am, Tuesday at 11:00 am, and Friday at 3:00 pm. You ask them to call you back and let you know which time works for them, and if none of these times work, you ask them to share some possible times they are available.

So, which of these two examples are you currently doing? Based on these two examples, which would you prefer receiving if you were the prospective client? Being specific is a simple way to make it easy for your clients to say *yes*.

Seeking Feedback

Feedback is an important part of rapport, and has so many opportunities to go awry.

When you think about the word *feedback*, does it have a positive or negative connotation? The word *feedback* is not a synonym for criticism.

Due to our instant-access society, giving and receiving feedback has become so much easier. At times, the number of people who want to weigh in and offer their opinion on what you're doing and saying can be overwhelming. With that in mind, here are a few do's and don'ts to keep the relationship intact and the rapport going.

Do: Let people know when they do something you appreciate. It's a huge rapport builder and encourages certain behaviors.

Don't: Use phrases like, "Can I be honest?" or "Honest piece of advice". Everything you say should be honest so don't use this type of qualifier unless everything else you say is a lie. These phrases actually create doubt about your integrity.

Do: Ask permission before offering feedback about something you don't appreciate. The one exception is when the behavior your pointing out is directly impacting you in some negative way. Anything else is just you forcing your opinion onto someone who didn't ask for it.

Don't: Speak for the masses or "all of us" unless you've been given specific permission by a particular group of people to do so.

Do: Keep your feedback specific to your own experience. It's much more credible when you talk from your own point of view.

Don't: Exaggerate or use throwaway lines (i.e., a million years, always, never). They diminish your credibility and may come off as condescending.

Do: Unsubscribe and unfollow people who have a message that doesn't resonate with you.

Don't: Imply that someone else's actions impact your own ability to be successful. It's a victim mentality and doesn't serve you.

Do: Move on once you've given your feedback.

Don't: Try to convince someone to agree with you. It's a waste of energy and not your job to force others to think like you.

Keep in mind, every time you feel the need to "give someone a piece of your mind," it has a ripple effect. The person you've put on blast knows people, has a voice, and may take this as permission to do the same to someone else. They may remember you and pass you over when they need what you offer. There's a myriad of other consequences that you can't even anticipate when giving unsolicited feedback.

Many of us grew up being told, "If you don't have anything nice to say, don't say anything at all." (Thanks, Bambi!)

Just because you can make your opinion known, doesn't mean you should. Before giving someone feedback, ask yourself, "What's the intention of offering this feedback?" When the intention is to embarrass, shame, or knock someone down, just don't.

When your intention is to help someone, lift them up, or make them aware of something so they'll have the opportunity to be/do better, then, by all means, reach out. Ask if they're open to receiving feedback from you. Once you have their permission to give feedback, kindly offer some advice.

Maintaining Rapport

Once the rapport bank account is open, we never stop making deposits. With every interaction I have with my clients, I'm on the lookout for ways to connect with them and avoid drawing from the account. Sometimes withdrawals are unavoidable. The goal of any stellar salesperson is to make sure the spaces between those withdrawals are filled with rapport-building activities.

Ways to Maintain Rapport

Where the behaviors around building rapport center around taking additive actions, maintaining rapport behaviors deals with actions we *shouldn't* take. Unlike finding new positive behaviors, identifying current rapport-damaging behaviors can sometimes be stressful. We don't like to admit that we've been doing something wrong!

Growth is a big part of scaling the Selling Staircase, and growth requires change. In this section, I ask that you keep an open mind as we go through these different methods of maintaining rapport.

Handling Awkward Encounters

Despite our focus on rapport, sometimes there are people we don't want to interact with. It's ok. It happens. But when you're forced to interact with someone you'd rather not, here are a few suggestions of what to do:

- First, determine how important is it to maintain a relationship with this person. When you need to keep things on good terms for the sake of your business, be willing to be the bigger person, and engage in a friendly conversation. Act as if all is well, and most of the time, the other person will go along with you.

- When the relationship is finished, maintain your professional composure. There's no reason be rude—yet don't be fake either. No need to put on a big production to try to make them feel at ease.
- Say hello when appropriate, and then move on and engage with the people you're there to connect with.
- For the people who want to hash it out, talk things to death, or otherwise steal your time, don't let them. These people do not get your attention. Attention includes your eyes, your time, and certainly your voice. They no longer have access to you.
- When you're approached by this person, say something generic like, "Hi, I hope you enjoy the event. Excuse me, there's someone I promised to connect with." Then walk away.

For those of us who were raised to be pleasant and always nice to others, it can be difficult to follow these steps. Yet, when you're prepared, you'll enjoy yourself more and be more strategic in your interactions.

I once read a great quote that says, "Cutting people out of my life doesn't mean I hate them; it simply means I respect myself."

Remember, you matter too, and you deserve consideration.

Protecting Your Reputation

Years ago, I worked for a company that was giving the sales team less than accurate information (though we didn't know it at the time) to pass along to our clients. When I asked a client who I had a previous relationship with to buy a new product, the information I passed along ended up blowing up in my face. My client was disgusted.

He felt so betrayed by me that he never spoke to me again. This was a powerful lesson. Even though I was passing along information that, to my knowledge, was accurate, the end result damaged *my* reputation.

I promised myself then that I would do everything I could to protect my reputation going forward, regardless if it cost me the sale.

Here are a few suggestions on how to ensure clients have only the best things to say about you behind your back:

1. Show up with integrity. Offer services and products of real value.
2. Be upfront and honest. If you can't deliver on your client's expectations, don't hide it. Tell them straight away.
3. Only promote the work of people who you've worked with yourself.
4. Only share accurate information about your results.
5. Be cautious about who you endorse or give testimonials and recommendations for.
6. For those who take pride in "telling it like it is" or giving your clients the "what for," chances are you're damaging the rapport. It's time to learn a softer and more diplomatic way to deliver information.

Due to my focus on teaching selling skills, people frequently share the horrible experiences they've had with someone in sales. It's interesting how often the same people's names come up again and again. Here are the behaviors people often use when describing the bad sales experience:

- Pushy
- Judgmental
- Abrasive
- Aggressive

- Terrible follow through
- Dishonest
- Unprepared

The counterexample (and how you might judge what people are saying about you) is when you show up at an event, and people say things like,

"So and so has the nicest things to say about you."

"I've heard so many great things about your program/services/product."

"I've been wanting to meet you."

When you're not getting any of the above comments, it might be time to do a little investigating. Ask a trusted colleague who you know will be candid, "What are people saying about me?" Be ready to take in the feedback—and hopefully learn from it.

Now, it's your turn. With the workbooks space below, list at least three people that you can turn to for candid feedback, then reach out to them and ask.

1. _____

2. _____

3. _____

This is a powerful exercise. Just because these trusted colleagues gave you candid feedback doesn't mean you have instant permission to do the same. Only offer it when it's requested. You might diminish rapport otherwise.

Stop Talking Down

Is there anything worse than someone who wants to sell you something and comes off as condescending?

Let's face it; nobody appreciates being talked down to. It's a huge rapport breaker, and if you're anything like me, people who come off as condescending don't get the business.

Yet, you might be surprised.

When you look back at your communication with clients, you may realize that some common language may come across as condescending or antagonistic. Chances are, this isn't your intent. These phrases are widely used in our society.

One phrase I've heard lately is, "What you don't know is . . ." (then the person tells you something about their product/service).

Umm . . . how do you know what they know or don't know? It's not a rapport builder to act like you know someone better than they know themselves. Another phrase that showed up in an email I received recently was, "It's important that you realize . . ." then the person told me something about their company.

My knee-jerk response was, "Important to who? You don't get to tell me what's important. I decide that for myself."

Are you starting to get a sense of how these phrases can come across as a little antagonistic or maybe even condescending?

What to do? Choose your words wisely when communicating with clients. Rephrase any statements that can be misconstrued as condescending or antagonistic.

Here are some examples of how to rephrase those statements above.

Statement 1: Instead of saying, "What you don't know is . . ." Consider using, "What you might be surprised to learn is . . ." or "What you might not know is . . ."

Statement 2: Instead of saying, "It's important that you realize . . ." Consider using, "What many clients find important is . . ." or "You may not have realized yet . . ."

Might, may, and *yet* are words frequently used in my communication. Adding *might* gives the statement a little wiggle room so you're no longer assuming what someone knows or doesn't know. You're simply offering information.

Dropping Terms of Endearment

Addressing clients with overly friendly terms like *honey, sweetie,* and *dear* may actually cause a withdrawal from your rapport bank account. Take a moment to answer this question: "How do you feel about a business contact using terms of endearments to address you?"

Maybe you're saying to yourself, "Depends on who it is and what they're calling me." Yeah, me too. A business contact that has known me for some time can get away with calling me just about any term of endearment, and I don't bat an eye. A business associate I've just met could damage their credibility with me by calling me these names.

For some, being called, *honey, sweetie,* or *dear* in a business environment is inappropriate and off-putting. Clients may choose to buy from someone else if you refer to them by these terms. So, eliminate these terms altogether in business situations.

Unfortunately, terms of endearment have become so commonplace that we forget to take into account how the other person perceives them. In the selling process, terms of endearment are rarely appropriate.

Instead, use your client's name. It's much easier to err on the side of being respectful versus an implied friendliness that your client may not feel or appreciate.

Recently, I had an experience with a vendor I hired to do some work for me. She knew my name and yet addressed all of her communication to me as, "Hello, dear . . ." My guess is that her intention was to come across as friendly and approachable. However, I found it uncomfortable and unprofessional. When a problem arose with the work, and she still addressed her email to me as, "Hello, dear," I felt disrespected and offended.

Building rapport and making deposits in the rapport bank account in each interaction is crucial to your success.

Stop Picking Brains

First, I want to go on record saying this is a terrible phrase. When people ask me this, my thought is always, "Yuck!" That's not what you want to have associated with your business. So, if you use the phrase, I would highly recommend you stop saying it.

Also, if you say this to people often . . . consider what you are actually asking. Do you keep going back to the well, asking for free advice in someone's area of expertise, and never paying them?

They've worked hard to earn their expertise, and their livelihood is built upon charging for that expertise. *Picking someone's brain* repeatedly, without being willing to pay them (especially when it is a service they charge for), is disrespectful and awkward.

If you are continually going to the same person for advice, consider hiring and actually paying them. You will likely get better information and will definitely stop deducting from the rapport balance.

Not everyone wants to swap or barter for services, so this isn't always a good offer either. While your expertise is great, they may not need it. Offering to trade secrets when they do not want/need the advice can cause resentment.

If you cannot afford to pay for the services, look into free options. Does that person have a blog, podcast, video series, Facebook page, or another free resource available? If they don't, it's likely someone has answered your question on the internet somewhere. Pick Google's brain instead! And, start making some deposits into the bank account of the people whose brain you have "picked" in the past to work on re-establishing rapport that might have been lost.

Safely Stepping Back

How do you feel about close talkers?

Your answer may depend on who the close talker is and how

much rapport they have with you. Have you ever struggled to stay in a conversation with a close talker even when it's an important client?

When my niece was ten, she asked me if it was ok to just yell, "Beep, beep, beep" and back away slowly when conversing with a close talker. (In case you're wondering, the short answer is *no*. Ha!)

One of my clients expressed the dilemma that she doesn't want to hurt the other person's feelings. Yet when someone is too close, she struggles to stay in the conversation. It requires too much energy and can be disruptive to her thinking process. She becomes overly focused on how close the other person is to her.

However big or small your personal space bubble is, you should give yourself permission to speak up when someone's making you feel uncomfortable. Your body, your rules. With that said, sometimes it's smart to have a subtle way to put some distance between you and the other person and still maintain the rapport.

The suggestion I gave my client is the same advice I gave my niece. When you want to maintain rapport and put distance between yourself and a close talker, do this:

1. Face the close talker
2. Take a step back on one foot
3. Leave the other foot out in front of you
4. Shift your weight to your back foot and lean back slightly
5. Continue on with the conversation as if nothing has changed

It's unlikely the close talker will get any closer to you than your front foot. This gives you some space and, hopefully, some breathing room. The stance may feel a little awkward, and yet it sends a subtle message to the close talker. You may even find they get the signal and back up.

When you send these subtle, nonverbal cues in a conversation, it's important to maintain your friendly demeanor. This lets the other person know you're still engaged and interested in the conversation and in them as a person.

Reviewing your Rapport-Maintaining Behaviors

Now, it's your turn. Let's take some of these behaviors and put them into practice. The following workbook questions are written to help with examining your rapport-maintaining behaviors, as well as address any brewing thoughts.

Look at your emails. Pay attention to the messages you leave on voicemail. How clear is it from the other person's perspective what to do next? How can you improve?

_____

_____

_____

_____

_____

Make a list of the last five to ten ideal clients that bought from you. Track back to where and how you earned their business. Did you meet them at a networking meeting? Were they referred to you? If so, by whom? Where did the lead come from? Like attracts like, so this is a great place to start. Go ahead and make your list here:

1. _____
2. _____
3. _____
4. _____
5. _____
6. _____
7. _____
8. _____

9. _____

10. _____

_____

_____

_____

_____

_____

Next, make a list of the last five purchases you've made for your business. How did you decide which person/company to buy from? How did you initially hear about the offering? How many times did you hear about it before making a buying decision? What, if anything, prompted you to move forward in the decision-making process?

1. _____

_____

_____

2. _____

_____

_____

3. _____

_____

_____

4. _____

_____

_____

5. _____

_____

_____

After making these lists, what, if anything, do they have in common? Any new insights for you? Where should you be spending your time, energy, and money to find new clients?

_____

_____

_____

_____

_____

Now, it's time to take action. Start scheduling time on your calendar to actively build relationships and sell. Most people never make time for this, and therefore, their business is not growing. Remember, the relationship must come first.

Once done, let's consider for the following workbook questions what you plan to do once you begin engaging with potential clients or appointments aimed at building relationships.

What are your goals for your next meeting?

_____

_____

_____

_____

CHAPTER 8
The Long Game

When's the last time you wanted something bad enough you were willing to put in the time and effort to make it happen?

Maybe it took weeks, months, or even years. Was it worth it when you finally reached your goal?

The selling process can sometimes require you to play the long game. Too often, people give up too early. People make up stories as to why they could never close the sale with XYZ company or earn the business of ABC person. I've had those same thoughts a time or two. We convince ourselves we're not capable, or that specific company or person would never want to work with us.

Frankly, when you give up too soon, you're proving your own theory correct. As the saying goes, "whether you think you can or think you can't . . . you're right." No company or person wants to work with someone who gives up easily.

People who've worked with me know I'm not a fan of chasing clients. I actually refuse to do it. Once a company or person has engaged me in a sales discussion and stops returning calls or emails, I gracefully let them know that when they're ready, I'd love to earn their business. At that point, I no longer actively pursue the sale.

However, that doesn't mean I don't believe in targeting specific clients. I do believe in creating a list of your ideal clients and then going about building a relationship to earn their business.

This relationship building is what I call playing the long game in the sales process.

Strive 5 List

My recommendation for playing the long game is to have at least five people on your list at all times. I call it the Strive 5 List. The list of prospects/connections will continue to change and need frequent updates. When you earn someone's business or get a hard *no*, then they come off the list, and you add someone new to the Strive 5.

By the way, this same process works when you're wanting to recruit people for your team and/or are looking for a job.

Here are the steps so you may do this too:

1. Create a list. Find companies or people you'd most like to work with. I teach this in my group coaching program known as Society Pro or "Prociety". Think big when making your list. What companies/people would bring influence and build recognition for you in your field? Which companies/people have the most potential for long-term profitable relationships?

2. Begin building a relationship. This might mean engaging with the company/person on social media and/or in person whenever possible. Do your research. Find out which organizations the people on your list belong to. Get involved and attend an event. Find out who you know on LinkedIn/Facebook that is connected to the person you want to work with. Ask your connections to make an introduction.

The relationship part of the process doesn't mean going in for the sale on your first interaction. There's nothing worse than having someone connect with me on LinkedIn/Facebook only to receive a message asking me to buy from them. Yuck.

No relationship almost always means no sale.

3. Test the waters. Once you've established rapport and started building the relationship, test the waters. Let the person know how much you'd like to work with them. Notice, I didn't say ask them for their business. You can say to someone, "You are my ideal client; I'd love to work with you." You're testing the water with this statement, seeing what they say next. When they want to know more, your opportunity for asking for the business is right around the corner. When they brush off your comment or change the subject, be willing to let it go, and focus on relationship building.

As you keep building the relationship, opportunities to test the water will come back around. Many times, a *no* from someone in this scenario is just a *not yet*.

Now, it's your turn.

First, in the workbook area below, write down your Strive 5 list:

1. _____
2. _____
3. _____
4. _____
5. _____

Next, begin to research possible ways to connect with them. In the workbook area below, note one possible way to begin building your relationship with them:

1. _____
2. _____
3. _____
4. _____
5. _____

I've applied these steps over and over again and been able to work with some of the companies/people that I initially tried to talk myself out of because I was afraid. Afraid they wouldn't think I was worth the money. I even used these steps many years ago to get hired at my ideal company. It took over two years of building relationships with key decision-makers in order to receive a job offer. In the end, playing the long game has always been worth it.

One of my favorite clients is actively engaged in playing the long game right now. She set her sights on a specific person she'd like to do business with. It's been fun to watch her create curiosity on social media about her business and engage her target client. It's almost like watching a finely choreographed dance.

Be strategic, make your list, and get working on it.

You've got this.

Finding the Sweet Spot

Have you ever noticed that when you're learning to do something new, you have to concentrate really hard in order to do it right?

And then as time goes by, and you've practiced a few times, it requires less concentration. Eventually, you can do it without having to really think about it. This is what's known as the *sweet spot*. It's easy and authentic—it's just how to show up in the world.

For many people, the idea of reaching the *sweet spot* when selling might seem unattainable. I'm going to let you in on a little secret— it's much easier than you think. The quickest and easiest way to reach the sweet spot is to make the relationship between you and the other person the priority.

At some point, you'll transition from focusing totally on the relationship to moving the conversation in the direction of doing business together.

When you start with the relationship first, it's much easier to broach the sales conversation. You don't have to be an expert salesperson with every tip and technique up your sleeve. Because of this book, you now know enough about the Selling Staircase to recognize what step you're on and what to do next.

One of my VIP clients recently had a huge realization about how she's been overlooking the relationships she's spent years developing. I tasked her with reaching out to key people in her network as a business-building activity, and people are thrilled to hear from her. More importantly, they are excited to help her build her business. By the way, the people she has relationships with are working for some of the most recognizable companies in the world.

Relationship selling always comes back to the relationship. People want to know you care about them. When they feel genuinely cared for, they're happy to help you regardless of the company name and title on their business card.

Create Authentic Connections

You may have heard of the concept of finding your client's pain point and focusing on that in order to close business. This is certainly a popular strategy. When used correctly, it does close business.

Unfortunately, there are too many people out there that have misinterpreted how to successfully utilize this technique. What I'm hearing and experiencing a lot is people creating pain points for prospects and then selling themselves as the solution.

The best analogy I can give is someone taking a piece of paper and making a bunch of small cuts up and down your arms and then saying to you, "Bless your heart, you're bleeding. I can help you with that." In these instances, I want to yell, "Yeah, I'm bleeding because you just cut me. I was fine before we started talking."

Someone once said to me, "It must be so easy for you to get clients, Nikki. You hear someone talk, and you know they suck at sales, so you can just tell them how much they need your services."

I was mortified that anyone would think I would say to someone, "You suck at sales, so hire me." In no way is that method making the relationship the priority! And, as you know, relationships are the foundation of my entire selling approach.

When people share their struggles with me about how hard they find selling, I ask questions, suggest tips (when requested), and, when appropriate, I offer my services as a way to help them get what they want. I'll never be the "tough love" kind of coach. Although, one of my clients does refer to me as the velvet hammer. However, the velvet hammer only shows up after you've hired me to support you in becoming better at selling. Tearing people down in order to build them up seems like a narcissistic, self-serving, and out-of-integrity approach.

Oh yes, this brings out my extra-large soapbox.

A woman proudly told me that one of the ways she sells her product (she sold accessories) is she would approach a woman in a coffee shop, compliment her outfit, and then tell her how her handbag really wasn't doing anything for her. I asked her if that worked as a sales strategy, and she proudly told me it had worked. I then asked her how much repeat business she receives, and her face fell. Turns out, few people bought a second time around.

Geez, I'll bet you can guess why people weren't buying from her a second or third time. Making people feel bad about themselves so you get their business is a terrible long-term strategy.

By the way, that woman is no longer in business.

Building long-term client relationships is a much more effective strategy.

Think about what it's like to spend time with someone who makes you feel good about yourself. Have you ever had a friend/mentor that sees the absolute best in you, and because of it, you elevate, grow, and push yourself to be better? It's a true gift to spend time with someone who makes you feel this way.

Are you that person for your clients? How might your relationships improve if this was the attitude you showed up with when meeting prospects? Do you think this would draw people to you? Would it be easier to close sales when people are vying to be around you?

Of course, this doesn't mean you can't have the difficult and sometimes hard to hear conversations with clients/prospects. However, these difficult things are better said when you have permission and when it will benefit them. Build rapport, develop the relationship, and ask permission before putting on your expert hat and pointing out places for improvement.

What to do? Create authentic connections with clients. Take time to learn about what's important to them before pitching them on your product/service or offering feedback/criticism. Prioritizing the relationship is where you find the sweet spot when closing sales.

Final Thoughts

Hopefully, you have had several *ah-ha* moments while reading *The Selling Staircase*. I hope you will act on them and see significant positive changes in your business.

Often, the frustrating thing about big realizations is that they seem obvious, or sometimes people have been saying some version of these concepts to you for years before they registered.

I had one a few years after starting my business, and I am sharing it with you in hopes that it will help you get over the hump of any pieces of advice in this book that were a little hard to read.

For two full years, clients were telling me a bit of information that I needed to know, and I kept dismissing the suggestion. Now, don't get me wrong; I listened to what they had to say and appreciated their input. Yet . . . I had a whole laundry list of why I didn't need to implement their suggestion.

What I was doing was working, so why change?

Then, an opportunity came up. In order to deliver a particular training, I had to implement the very suggestion people had been giving me for years. I'll sheepishly admit that not only was the training tremendously better for the participants, but I've never gone back to my "old way" again. I freaking loved it. It fulfilled me in ways I can't begin to describe.

So now, please allow me to challenge you for a moment and ask, "What have people been suggesting to you over and over again (perhaps something you skimmed over in this book . . .) in regard to your business that you've been dismissing?"

Consider putting some deep thought around your true reason for not taking the suggestion. Is it pride, ego, shame, overwhelm, or lack of knowledge holding you back? In my case, it was shame.

The suggestion clients kept giving me was to see me during virtual trainings that I had always taught as a teleclass. When people asked why I didn't offer my trainings as webinars (seems silly to think that just a few short years ago, teleclasses were more common than webinars), I had a list of reasons that sounded valid and well thought out. However, the truth was that I hate seeing myself on camera. It's uncomfortable and kind of embarrassing. My inner critic has a lot to say when I have to watch myself on camera, and frankly, my inner critic can be incredibly cruel.

Even though I don't love it, I'm willing to be uncomfortable and embarrassed when it makes the experience for the client better. As I have said before, relationship selling is about the client, not about you (or, in this case, me). As soon as I realized the clients' experience was better, I was totally sold. As it turns out, my experience was better because I was no longer focused on what I looked like on camera, I was focused on the participants in the training. Being able to see their facial expressions was priceless.

Now, it's your turn. I know it's scary, and remember, these notes are just for you. Be honest with yourself: What are clients consistently asking for that you have yet to give them? Answer the question in the workbook area below:

_____

_____

_____

_____

Put some effort into giving their suggestion a try, and see how it impacts your business. For the suggestions that make a positive impact on your bottom line, consider implementing them long-term.

It's easy to get caught up in thinking, "Why would I change what appears to be working?" (The "if it ain't broke, don't fix it" mentality.) What you may not be considering is how much better things could be if you implemented what your clients are asking for. Maybe things are broken, and you don't even realize it.

When multiple people are saying the same thing to you, it's time to get out of your own way. You may be costing yourself business if you continue to ignore this.

You Are Not Alone

We're at the end of the book, and the beginning of your new sales experience. Thank you for purchasing this book and spending this time with me!

Before you go, there are just a few more things to share with you.

First of all, I believe in you. I know you can ascend the Selling Staircase and find success for yourself and your clients.

Second, remember that the foundation of successful relationship selling is built on rapport. If you're feeling overwhelmed or unsure of how to take all of this into your business, start with rapport. If you're building trust and rapport, you're in a good place.

Third, you don't have to sell like anyone else. (This is why learning the steps to selling is crucial.) Once you know the steps, you can add minor tweaks to your approach and still see success in the way you sell. Be yourself. The calmer and more authentic you are, the easier it will be for you and your client.

Most importantly—you are not alone.

There is more support available to you. I'm here to help with any of your relationship selling needs. You're also warmly invited to join the Sales Maven Society.[6] This is my community of brilliant profes-sionals just like you who are committed to honing their selling skills. It would be my honor to support you in building long-lasting rela-tionships as well as bringing more revenue into your business.

---

6   To be a part of this amazing group, go to: https://yoursalesmaven.com/society/

Acknowledgments

A special thank you to Melina Palmer for helping me get clear on the book I most wanted to write this time around. Your friendship and advice are priceless.

To Katie Cross and her team—you all are AMAZING. You made this experience fun, and I appreciate all the hand-holding you had to do to get this book to market. I'm so grateful and will be singing your praises for years to come!

To my clients, thank you for allowing me to be on this journey with you. I have to pinch myself often because I'm so blown away by the caliber of people that hire me.

A special thank you to all of the people who gave me stories to share in this book—you continue to provide me with ideas for how to do it better.

Thank you for reading this book. I'm deeply grateful for the time you invested.

About the Author

Nikki Rausch has a passion for the art of selling—and it shows.

She is the founder and CEO of Sales Maven, an organization dedicated to authentic selling. Her unique ability is to transform the misunderstood process of "selling" into techniques, tools, and tips that can be successfully incorporated into a process by anyone.

Nikki has received numerous sales awards, shattered sales records across industries, and was featured in Female Entrepreneur Magazine. A sought-after speaker, she regularly shares the results of success through illuminating keynote addresses and business-changing workshops. Her robust Sticky Selling Master Academy ignites game-changing outcomes for clients, many of whom have also reaped the benefits of her immersive VIP consultations.

Nikki shares her knowledge on a wide range of sales topics. Her popular book, *Buying Signals* is available on all online retailers. *Six-Word Lessons on Influencing with Grace* can be found on Amazon.

References

1. Baer, Drake. 2015. "Science Says People Decide These 13 Things within Seconds of Meeting You." Business Insider. Business Insider. November 18, 2015.
   http://www.businessinsider.com/science-of-first-impressions-2015-11

2. Lebowitz, Shana. 2016. "Turns out It's Nearly Impossible to Get Past a Bad First Impression." Business Insider. Business Insider. December 12, 2016.
   https://www.businessinsider.com/first-impressions-matter-more-than-we-think-2016-12

Made in the USA
Lexington, KY
06 December 2019

57999535R00068